NO ONE IS PEEING IN THE DEEP END

A Survival Guide for Launching a Dream

SHANNON CROTTY

Disclaimer

The information in this book is based on the author's knowledge, experience and opinions. The methods described in this book are not intended to be a definitive set of instructions. You may discover other methods and materials to accomplish the same end result. Your results may differ.

This book is not intended to give legal, financial, or psychological advice and is sold with the understanding that the author is not engaged in rendering legal, accounting, or other professional services or advice. If legal or financial advice or other expert assistance is required, the services of a competent professional should be sought to ensure you fully understand your obligations and risks.

For Brian

All deep-end dreamers need a place to rest and breathe, a place to be seen and understood, a place to be respected and loved, and a place to feel believed in.

You have always been and continue to be that place for me.

My favorite place on earth is wherever you are. I love you so much.

TABLE OF CONTENTS

Part Three: Your Dream and Other People

INTRODUCTION

I remember the exact moment I said it. It was in the bathroom.

It was only a few years into Polka Dot Powerhouse's journey, and I was sitting smack dab in the middle of sheer terror mode. To the outside world, everything looked wonderful. I was the leader of a rare success story—we were one of the few companies to catch fire and gain not only loads of customers and members, but also a substantial national following. I was so proud of all we had accomplished, but I was still trying to find my feet, and I was not entirely sure it all was really happening or even how it had happened in the first place.

I had just given my "founders" keynote speech at the annual conference we hold for our amazing members, and we had then been dispersed for a much-needed bathroom break.

I headed for the bathroom for the normal reasons but also to find a moment to gather myself. My normal practice after I speak is to find a quiet place to rein in my mind and emotions after revealing myself to a roomful of people. Sometimes it's back in my hotel room, and other times, it's an unused conference room. That day, it was in stall three of the conference level women's bathroom.

I selfishly and silently hogged stall three as women came in and out. Having already finished my official bathroom business, with my pants back on, I sat there silently. I needed a few minutes alone, and I was willing to wait patiently for it. As women flowed in and out of the bathroom, I listened lovingly to their conversations and smiled, reveling in the fact that our company brought all these women together. After ten or fifteen minutes, the bathroom quieted again, and I found my opportunity to exit the stall, believing everyone had left.

As I washed my hands, I looked in the mirror and reconfirmed that, once again, I was okay. I had survived even though I had been the focus of hundreds of pairs of eyes. I had spoken from the heart and with authenticity, and the floor had not gobbled me up. I stood there for a moment, staring at myself as if to say, "See, you're okay. You've got this."

My focus was shattered by the sound of a flushing toilet. Oops! I had missed one. I was no longer alone.

A Polka Dot sister exited stall five. I knew of her, but I didn't know her well. She was a fairly new member. Beautiful, smart, and kind.

The normal pleasantries ensued. "How is your day going?" "Good. Yours?"

Normal bathroom small talk.

Then she asked, "How did you do it?"

I answered with something like, "One step at a time—just making the next best move and trusting it would all work out."

"No," she responded. "How did you keep going when it all looked like it had failed? How did you keep going when you wanted to quit?"

Ooh… she wanted the down and dirty. She didn't want the magic pill to success; she wanted the key to survival. "No one is peeing in the deep end," I replied. "When you're doing something big, you don't have time for nonsense. Truthfully, being in the deep end and having to learn to swim is what saved me."

That was the first time I had heard that saying, and I could barely believe it came out of my own mouth. "No one is peeing in the deep end." Where had that come from?

As I decompressed in the days after the conference, I returned to reflect on that phrase.

My thoughts took me back to my beliefs about the shallow end and deep end of the water.

I am a visual learner. If you want an idea to stick into my head, you'd better have a specific, fun, or unique visual that I can link it to. I don't need you to show me the visual on a screen; I need you to give me a visual shortcut to refer back to in my head. That's the way I learn, and that's the way I present as well. It's no surprise that I was led to see a vivid visual of this phrase.

For me, I see the shallow end as fun and relaxing; I've always related the shallow end to playing. It's where there's a lot of jubilance: kids in floaties, yelling and screaming, with beach balls being thrown back and forth. It's a place for beginners or possibly people who just want to chill and soak up the sun. It's a wonderfully joyous place, and thinking of the shallow end makes me smile. And, truth be told, the shallow end is where kids may be tempted to pee.

The deep end, on the other hand, is on a completely different level, and it is not a place for fun and games. When I think of the deep end, I think of focus, intention, and additional risk. Generally, being in the deep end means you mean business, and you're going to have to work a bit harder than you may have had to in the shallow end. You're going to have to take it up a notch, and it'll require courage and a hell of a lot of focus and strength to survive a swim in the deep end.

I've always heard about people being thrown into deep water and learning to swim in order to avoid drowning. I think that sounds a lot like what it means to launch a dream—equal parts scary and exhilarating. I know someone is going to read this and say to me, "Yes, but what if you have to *go*? I bet there's pee in the deep end, too!" Yes, I am sure occasional peeing happens in the deep end by necessity, but my point is no one is doing much in the deep end that would require them to pull from their focus. People don't venture to the deep end to splash around and play.

I often use that visual to relate to launching a dream. To be in the shallow end of launching a dream is fun and beautiful—that's where the newness of a dream feels big and fresh and sparkly! However, the shallow end is also where a person talks about it, reads about others doing it, thinks about it, and plans to do it *someday*. To be in the deep end of launching a dream means you're taking action, risking failure, and putting yourself in a place that is going to require a level of work and belief you've never experienced before. It means moving forward through the sheer darkness of the unknown at the risk of losing it all, feeling terrified because you have a dream that won't leave you alone, and knowing deep in your gut it is meant to impact the world. *That* is what it means to be in the deep end of launching a dream.

Launching a dream is no splash through the shallow end; it's a daunting journey. Only the bravest of the brave need apply. It is equal parts joy and struggle. Looking back, I feel a guidebook with helpful advice would have been nice for someone in the deep end. I now understand how impossible that is, since each dream and each founder is so unique. No two journeys are alike, and that's by design.

Still, there are so many things I wish people would have prepared me for as I stumbled into my role as an unlikely founder. After ten years, I set out to create what I hoped would be a warmly welcomed floatation device for current or future deep-end dream launchers.

I became the unlikely founder of Polka Dot Powerhouse in 2012. At the time, I owned a regional women's magazine. The magazine was a safe place for me. It allowed me to stay in the comfort of my own area. It also allowed me to get to know and interact with people but often only at arm's length, a comfortable distance that allowed me to safely control the situation. Then, suddenly, everything changed.

My beloved sister, Tina, who passed in 2010, had always been my lifeline to the world. She was my only and older sibling. Growing up, our home life was chaotic and troubling to say the least. My beautiful mom loved us and made sure we knew it, but she had her hands full juggling all the messes that constantly found their way into our lives. While it became the norm for us to hide behind the camouflage of the "everything is fine" fiction in public, I could put away the façade for Tina. I could let my guard down and allow myself to feel when she was with me. Tina was my protector, the one and only person who I could truly breathe with while we were growing up. Truthfully, she was my first and, for many years, only healthy relationship with another human. She was and continues to be one of the foundational pillars of my life.

When she died unexpectedly, it changed everything for me overnight. I know she is always with me, and I consult with her often through prayer and meditation. So many of my decisions in life seemed focused on what Tina would do. So, back in 2012, after enduring a difficult period, and when I pulled my car off the highway and bawled on the side of the road, praying to Tina for guidance and wisdom, she delivered the name Polka Dot Powerhouse into my brain. I didn't know what it meant then, but it turned out to be one of the greatest gifts of all time.

Initially, Polka Dot Powerhouse looked like a complete failure; we only had one person sign up on launch day, and it was only that one paid member for the first two months of our existence. But once we made it past the first few months and started to find some traction, I started to think about what would be expected of me as the founder. The problem was all the founders of global companies whom I was exposed to at that time were the well-known, famous people who looked as though they had either been birthed into a big spotlight for their role or gone to special founder school for it. They were all perfect. *Perfect!* Perfectly dressed, perfectly spoken, perfectly experienced and knowledgeable, perfectly crafted… or so it seemed.

I thought I was missing something, so I would google things like, "What does a founder say, wear, eat?" I was disappointed to not find much at all. I had even started a Pinterest page for all the wonderful insight I planned to find, but there was nothing to save. No such information existed. That was horribly inconvenient for someone like me who knew nothing about what they were doing. I wanted someone—anyone—to guide me. I wanted it, yet I couldn't ask for it. What if they knew I didn't know what I was doing? What if everyone found out? What if they saw me? So, I slapped on a smile and tried to camouflage my worries, my insecurities, and my ignorance. I went on, operating in a very public role yet hiding as much as I could. It was a miserable way to live.

Now, after many years of reading business biographies, I've learned that very seldom does a company or a founder get birthed to perfection. Despite how easy it looks from the outside, most of the time there is a great deal of struggle, challenges for growth, and hard hits on the foundation of their successes. You may not see it, and sometimes it's fun to pretend it's as easy as it looks, but the struggle is there. It's not what the general public or even those with big dreams are shown, and that's a good thing. No one wants to air their dirty laundry for the world, and the world doesn't want or really need to see that either. It's on a "need to know" basis, and you know who needs to know? That's right! The founders of the present and future.

I believe if the leaders of the present can at least be truthful about what it looks like, on a personal level, to launch a dream, it will help those going through it right now and those who will go through it in the future. Talking about it and sharing our stories is a confirmation that we aren't broken, that we aren't doing it wrong. Obstacles are part of the process—an important part. It will all make sense looking back.

Sometimes when I talk to a fellow founder, and we compare notes on a current struggle, one of us will say, "Yeah, no one talks about that." My question is, why not?

This book is the book I wish I had read when we first started, not to make the road any easier or simpler, but so I could have known that almost every founder goes through these challenges at one time or another. It's a rite of passage of sorts, and it's completely normal. We aren't in the wrong place. The dream wasn't sent to the wrong person. We're not doing it the wrong way. In fact, we're probably doing it just right.

I am writing this as a personal survival guide for those currently in the deep end with me and those currently entering the water or thinking about it—someone who is just starting to dip a toe in.

Even though most of us are full of big dreams, many people don't take action to make them a reality. The list of reasons people don't dare to swim in the deep end is long. And it's their business. But one thing is for sure: This business of going to the deep end to launch a dream can be so scary and full of obstacles that anyone courageous enough to take that dive deserves the respect of hearing what it may truly look like. Knowledge is power. Knowledge through someone else's experience can be the life vest we occasionally need in order to keep on swimming.

Success breeds challenges, challenges breed muscles, and muscles breed strength. To be in the deep end of launching a dream is a big undertaking. We must celebrate it as such with truth, honesty, and authenticity. The world needs more of that.

What you won't find in this book are growth graphs, scaling tactics, or industry secrets. There are excellent books about growing and scaling your business if that's what you need.

This book is all about you, the founder, the keeper of the dream. It's about feeling seen, knowing about some of the challenges that may be coming, and allowing yourself to be supported by the knowledge that we all go through some version of the same journey. We all pay to play in the deep end. The challenges are the price of admission for something as rewarding as launching a dream that impacts people.

This book includes twenty-six survival tips I have gathered throughout my journey. Within each survival tip, you will discover both an opportunity for growth and a reason to celebrate. I encourage you to search for those along your founder journey as you read this book.

So, follow me to the deep end of launching a dream, and remember, no one is peeing in the deep end.

Part One

THE DREAMER – THAT'S YOU

CELEBRATE THE GIFT OF BEING A VISIONARY

You're more special than you think.

I'll be the first to tell you that I had no intentions of being the visionary of Polka Dot Powerhouse. The whole thing was way beyond my comfort zone. Many days it still is. But I really had no choice. It's how I'm built.

I was always the crazy idea person. I was, at all times, juggling five or six catchy names that had no obvious purpose. There is a funny meme on social media about women having fifty mental tabs open at all times. Ha! Fifty sounds like rookie level to me. I always had about two hundred mental tabs open at all times, all full of beautiful sparks of exciting ideas with no obvious destinations. I'm not saying I recommend this as the most efficient system in the world, but it's mine and I have learned to stand unapologetically in gratitude of it.

Truthfully, I believe I annoy more people than I actually impress with my visionary abilities. Many people can't relate to me, and that's okay. I'm not meant to please everyone in the world. I am meant to change the world in a very specific way that no one else has changed it yet. And that big truth scares people. People are scared of what they don't understand, and a dream visionary can be a confusing animal for those who aren't built with the same strengths. Visionaries push the limits, and we challenge the way things have always been done in order to do something new. That's beyond scary for people—it can be downright terrifying. But that's okay, too. The visionary keeps moving forward anyway.

The fact that you picked up this book likely means you're a visionary, too—a visionary of ideas, a visionary of dreams, a visionary of impact to the world. If you weren't a visionary, you probably wouldn't have even noticed this book or thought the image of me under water (I was really photographed under water, by the way) was weird or too "out there." But you bought it or borrowed it from a friend, or perhaps you were given it as a gift from someone who sees a spark in you. Everything happens in perfect timing. You, the visionary of an amazing idea and dream, were meant to read this book.

While I may not know you personally, I do know exactly who you are. You see things in a way many others don't. You may even feel differently than other people. That feeling is right; you are different. For me, that often felt like a bad thing, but the truth is it's an incredible gift.

Every human is unique and has been given their unique strengths and so-called "weaknesses" for a reason. We are each here to impact the world in very specific and wonderful ways, and we've been built to do just that.

The true idea or dream visionary is a somewhat rare creature. A visionary gets an idea, and their brain shoots it forward into the future, usually with no end in sight. Sure, everyone has goals and aspirations, but for a visionary of a dream, it is different. They see it differently than the rest of the world. Sometimes it's crystal clear, and other times it can be a bit hazy, but either way, the line of vision is ultimately at a level others cannot relate to.

For a visionary, the dream simply won't leave them alone. They may want it to go away, to be quiet, or to go to someone else instead, but it's not going to happen that way. The dream they carry and the vision of it will haunt them until they make a move, and it will continue to occupy a lot of their mind space until it reaches the destination they are meant to take it to.

Visionaries often stay up late and get up early, working with a mind that won't leave their vision alone. They dream of it. The dream they hold (and sometimes they hold many) is almost a second version of themselves in that it is always there, poking them, jumping up and down for attention, and begging to be seen.

Look into a visionary's eyes, and you're very likely to see an extra little sparkle. Big ideas create sparks that shine into everything they do.

Being a visionary is more than a strength. It's more than a possibility or having potential. Being a visionary of a beautiful dream and being strong enough to take action on it tells me you are an extraordinarily designed human who has a real capability to improve the world and positively impact so many countless humans in it. You are something special, and that is worth celebrating.

An Opportunity for Growth

Being a visionary can mean being different than others around us. The work for us visionaries can include making sure we see and embrace all of ourselves and the value we have for the world, as well as the way we will impact it.

A Reason to Celebrate

Being a visionary means you've been entrusted to bring value and impact into the world. That's definitely a reason to celebrate.

JUST BE YOU AND THEN BE YOU A LITTLE MORE

You are a complete package. All you need to be is more of you.

The first few years of Polka Dot Powerhouse's existence were full of fears and doubts for me—the fear of being found out as someone who was not supposed to be in this role or the fear someone else would come along and tell me I had possibly been doing it wrong the whole time. So many fears. It's a wonder I got anything done. It's a wonder Polka Dot took off at all. I wasted a lot of the joy of that time by being consumed with fear. If only I had realized the key to so much of our success and many others is being more of ourselves. I wouldn't change one thing about our journey, but if I could go back to the first three or four years and talk to that younger founder, I would say, "Girl, be more of yourself, and the rest will fall into place."

There's so much pressure put on the keeper of the dream—pressure to do all the things, pressure to be good at all the things, or pressure to look as though we have it all together and do everything with perfection, skill, and style. So much stinkin' pressure! I see you, my fellow founder, and I know you have so much pressure on you.

Pressure is not always a bad thing—look at the diamond. There's so much beauty from so much pressure. Humans are different. Humans take things personally and carry so much guilt and shame around from feeling they are not able to be everything for everyone at the right time, all the time.

People like to point to social media as the culprit for all of our pressure. Sure, it's part of the equation, but I do not think it bears full responsibility for this pressure we feel.

I think a bigger factor may be that leaders, feeling the immense pressure they do, aren't honest enough about the journey. They feel a constant expectation to be perfect, and why wouldn't they? Not only are customers, clients, investors, and the public looking at us to do it all right and look and sound perfect while we do, but the leaders we are leading are also looking to us to be the answer to every single issue, every complaint, and every strongly worded suggestion. Not only are we comparing ourselves to other leaders, but others are, too. Sally over at this company does it this way or that way. That customer might be seeing Sally's highlight reel, but they may not have any clue what it's really like for Sally as a leader. If we're going to judge our behind-the-scenes to other's highlight reels, or if we're going to act as if others are holding us to that standard, we're going to feel pretty lousy. That's exactly what is happening to leaders right now.

I'm a big fan of leaders who are honest and authentic about what it looks like to launch a dream, not in broadcasting every trial and struggle and not in airing their dirty laundry, but in being brave enough to show it's not about being perfect. It never has been. Launching a dream is more about mistakes than success. It's about the strength to keep moving forward, even though you may be able to see only a few feet ahead. The truth of that can be scary to share. People want you to be authentic until you are and then they sometimes want you to go back to perfection. They want you to be authentic but not too real. You cannot be authentic and meet perfection expectations at the same time. They cannot exist together. Because your not-so-perfect reality as a founder is seen as less desirable to the public, you may start to feel conflicted about your role as the keeper of the dream; you may start to doubt yourself and wonder if you jumped into the wrong deep end.

The truth is that you are perfect just as you are, even if your "perfect" doesn't look so perfect to someone else. The areas you shine in are designed to fit you for a reason. The areas you may struggle in? They're there for a reason, too. There are no mistakes. You are not broken. You're not doing it wrong. You are the perfect representation of what you're meant to do on this earth and how you're meant to impact people and the world. Let that sink in for a minute.

Go to a mirror and look into your own eyes. Give yourself a smile, but don't lose contact with those eyes. That wondrous beauty you are looking at is a masterpiece that was designed perfectly for what makes your heart shine and for what will help you make the world a better place. But you have to start believing it to truly get into the zone.

Sometimes, to gain more clarity, you simply need to see things in a new way. You need the see the perfection of what is. You see, if you were sent the gift of an incredibly impactful dream, you are the *perfect* person to move that dream forward. Everything about you—the strengths, the so-called "flaws," all of it—is perfect for taking things to the next step, or it would have been sent to someone else.

If you can learn to break free from the old story of what a founder and keeper of the dream looks like and accept the new story—the truth that you are perfect for this dream—and if you can learn to be more of yourself by embracing everything that makes you special, unique, and different, it will make the journey less stressful and a lot more fun.

An Opportunity for Growth

There is the tendency for a keeper of the dream to be told to be this or that. It is your job as a visionary and leader to learn to stifle the outside noise and be more of yourself, so you can do your work.

A Reason to Celebrate

You've got everything you need inside of you to make this happen. Insert happy dance!

Survival Tip #3

USE THE POWER OF THE NINETY-SEVEN PERCENT SUCK RATE

You and I both suck at ninety-seven percent of things, thank goodness.

Back when I ran the magazine that Polka Dot Powerhouse was launched under, we had so much fun. We did a lot of silly things and called it work. We had a catch phrase for our staff and readers: "What would whimsy do?" That was our driving force. We certainly had plenty of stress and challenges, and we had days that made us question whether it was all worth it. However, we conducted business with that whimsical outlook, and it was so much fun. At vendor events, we played practical jokes on other vendors or attendees; we randomly picked days to put money under windshields or take flowers to people working drive-through windows or to people paying for gas at the gas station. Yes, we actually published a magazine, too, but we made sure to feed our own souls in the process, which was a wonderful place to be.

Everyone is looking for more joy in life. Because we had so much fun, we had an endless supply of people who asked how they could become more than a reader, how they could become part of our crew instead. "How can I be a bigger part of this? How can I help?" became frequent questions from some of the regular readership that we saw at events. My answer was always the same. "I don't know. What do you love to do?"

The question often confused people. "No. I mean what do you need?" And again, I would reply, "I don't know. What do you love to do?"

Most of the time, people never gave me an answer. They often walked away stunned, not sure I had understood them. I had. I wasn't playing mind games with them. I know with everything in me that if people don't get to consistently work, play, and live in their zones of genius, they will never be happy or fulfilled in what they do.

Buckle up because I'm getting ready to lay down a big truth. You and I and all the people of the world suck (or are only so-so) at approximately ninety-seven percent of things.

It's true! I believe you only have a very small percentage where your zone of genius lives—that space where you are so dang good at something that it's almost second nature. For most people it's a very, very small percentage of the things they do most days; for some, it's even less than three percent.

When I'm at events and bring up the power of the ninety-seven percent suck rate, I will frequently have someone walk up to me afterward and say something like, "I know that's true for most people, but I'm really good at all the things." Oh, I don't think so. I always respond with love, "I think you're lying to yourself."

True, you may have had to learn to be able to do a lot of things. Humans are so amazing and can evolve to gain skills to help us do what we need to do. Most founders and visionaries start out wearing all the hats and doing everything and handling all the tasks, even if it's not in their strength set. That's fine. You do what you have to do. I do that, too, but that's not what I'm talking about. I'm talking about your zone of genius—the things you could do and talk about doing all day. It's what you do that makes you feel more like yourself. It's a small percentage of your overall skills; it's the high-level genius and talent you have that others possibly don't understand—the small part of what you do that brings you the most happiness and the part that seems to have the biggest impact on people.

I'll give you an example. I am a visionary with zero detail skills. *Zero.* Sure, I'm a human, so I can do detailed things. I've done them, and I continue to do them on a daily basis. I do them because I have to, but it's not my zone of genius. And because detail work is not my zone of genius, I do these tasks at a snail's pace which makes them even less desirable. These things I am capable of doing but are not what I was built for distract me from my zone of genius.

Frequently, someone on our upper leadership level of Polka Dot Powerhouse (we call them Legacy Leaders) will send me a very detailed email, and I start to get a little nauseated as I begin to read. I find myself speed-reading through it and searching for the question marks. Anyone else? No? Just me? Okay. One paragraph in, I am likely already lost and still searching for that darn question mark. Most of the time, if I can't quickly figure out what they need from me, I shut down and convince myself to come back and figure it out later. Sometimes that happens, and other times it does not. The times it doesn't, I'll often get an email saying something to the effect of, "I see from your lack of response that I've put too many details in my email, so here's a summary." Yes! Now *that* I can get behind.

While my inability to handle a lot of details may appear, to most people, to be a flaw—something about me that seems "less than" to be corrected, or at least hidden, from the world—I know better. My journey with Polka Dot Powerhouse has taught me many things about others and about myself. Maybe the most important lesson I have learned is I can impact the world at an astonishing level, if only I learn to accept myself and use the talents I was given. I can more easily get to my zone of genius and stay there longer if I just stay in my lane. I do not need to be, nor was I meant to be, good at all the things, and neither were you. We were all designed perfectly for what we're meant to do on this earth. While we may have areas we would *like* to improve on, there are no areas that *need* be fixed to positively impact the world.

Sometimes when I bring this up, someone will ask me how I think the areas of myself that may have seemed out of place have actually helped the Polka Dot Powerhouse community. Maybe the fact that I'm a type A, rigid personality and have high standards and firm boundaries has helped us spread. Maybe being a commander with an unwavering mindset helped me maintain the strength to carry on when someone else may have given up. I can't tell you exactly how I helped us grow, spread, and thrive, but I know that the dream was placed in my heart, and its pull was strong enough for me to take action for a reason.

Even though I wasn't sure what I was doing for a long time, and I lived in total terror that someone would find out I wasn't good enough, I now trust that nothing is moving out of time; there are no accidents or mistakes. The dream was given to me, and I was meant to lead it, even with what others feel are my flaws. The same is true for you. No one can take that away from you, this immense gift you have been given.

An Opportunity for Growth

You stink at ninety-seven percent of things by design, and that concept flies in the face of everything society has taught us. Work to make peace with that, and embrace your so-called flaws for what they are—more of what makes you, you!

A Reason to Celebrate

Sucking at ninety-seven percent of things means you can release those things to focus on your three percent of genius. That three percent of genius will truly impact the world.

SEE YOUR FLAWS AS YOUR SUPERPOWERS

You are uniquely you. "Flaws" is just another way to say "unique."

So, how do you take this total package you've been given—this beautiful creation that is you—and use it as a force of good in a way that impacts the world? How do you reconcile your feelings of inadequacy in a way that literally propels your dream into the world? I'll tell you one thing that has worked really well for me. I learned to see my flaws as my superpowers. I'll say that one again—I learned to see my flaws as my superpowers.

I am a very impatient person. I have no patience at all. It annoys almost everyone, but that's not my problem. Sometimes it even annoys me, too. I look at people who seem to have so much patience, and I sometimes think how nice it would feel to be like them. How nice it would be to have the ability to wait patiently for great things and be so relaxed about it that I almost forget about it. That sounds absolutely wonderful, and I am a bit envious of people who can do that, but only for a minute. More often than not, the thought of being patient feels like science fiction to me and makes me more than a little queasy. I don't understand it at all. That's not how I'm built. It's not how my brain is wired, and it's not how my heart beats. I only understand action and forward movement. That is my happy place, and that's how I am geared. That's my zone of genius, the place from which I can best help and most powerfully impact the world.

I can tell you without a doubt that if I had any patience at all, we would have never launched Polka Dot Powerhouse—not a chance in the world. I would have overthought it to the point of failure. I would have questioned, and I would have stopped. If I were a person who had the strength of patience, I don't know where I would be today, but it wouldn't be here.

Being impatient is what lit the spark to start the women's magazine I owned, despite having no experience, and it's what gave me the determination to keep the Polka Dot Powerhouse flame going that was lit by our first member. It's also what is enabling me to write this book.

Being impatient is what others would call a flaw, and there are days when that's what I call it, too, but it is without a doubt my superpower because it enables me to take an idea, make the leap of announcing it, start to bring it to life, and figure it out as I go, sometimes in the complete darkness of ignorance.

This may not work for you or most other people, but it works for me. It is my superpower.

So, what's something you or others have perceived as a flaw about yourself, and how can you tilt your perspective of that to see it more clearly as what it's intended to be—your *superpower*?

There's no time like the present, so stop reading right now, and take a moment to list all of the things about you that are perceived "flaws," either by you or someone else. You'll know if someone else thinks one of your traits is a flaw because they'll have complained about it at some point. It may have even been something passed down as negative trait in your family. Maybe others haven't told you, but you've thought it (although I bet it started from hearing it somewhere; you weren't born with this feeling about yourself). If you had to find an aspect about each flaw that would actually help support this dream of yours, what would it be? How can you shift your perspective of each flaw into a superpower? The answer is there, sitting and waiting somewhere inside you.

I've found that when you spend less time feeling unworthy because of a perceived flaw, and when you find more ways to love yourself not as better than anyone else, but as perfectly built for being the human you are, you free up that load of time you previously spent in self-induced distraction. The time you would have spent being distracted by the constant loop of negativity your mind can play about "flaws" can better be served in launching and supporting your dream and impacting countless people.

Finding and embracing how flaws are superpowers is a long-term project. It may take you years to make peace with them, and practicing this may dredge up feelings you don't want to feel. You may even want to seek the support of a professional therapist to sort through your thoughts as you encounter them. However, this practice can completely transform how you spend your time. You'll spend less time in distraction and more time increasing your love for yourself. What you send into the world comes back to you. This is especially true for what you send yourself. The more ways you find to appreciate, respect, and love yourself, the more you'll have people showing up in your life who will also be able to appreciate, respect, and love themselves as well as you.

An Opportunity for Growth

We've been fed the lie that our weaknesses are reasons to be ashamed and are areas we need to improve. There is power in getting past that lie.

A Reason to Celebrate

You were built to perfection for what you are here to do. If you choose to change your perspective and look closely, you'll discover your so-called "flaws" are really your superpowers.

REALIZE THAT IT'S ALL MESSAGING

It's very simple. Everything you do and say is a message. No pressure.

I'm very excited we are on the subject of messaging because it's so important to your journey of launching and growing a dream.

We're constantly sending messages to ourselves and the rest of the world. In every moment, a message is being sent, and usually, there are many messages sent throughout the day, whether or not we realize it.

Whatever you believe in—God, the Universe, the Divine— just know that it is waiting for you to tell it what you want, what makes you happy, and what you wish to focus on more with your time.

The more ways you can find to understand and love yourself and others, the more ways it will come back to you; you'll also find more people who are able to do the same and be able to do it for you. Once you start working the muscles of seeing ways to love yourself, you will find more reasons and ways to love yourself.

You might be wondering why I am putting so much emphasis on messaging in a book about launching a dream. At some point along your journey, you'll realize that it's because it will literally become your lifeline. Launching a dream can be isolating at times, and you're going to need yourself as a loving ally every day, several times a day, for the rest of this journey. You will need to be your own best friend, the love of your life, and your own biggest cheerleader. It's not to say you won't need other people, because you definitely will. But, you will absolutely need to count on yourself first and foremost for the actions and feelings you seek from others. You will have to lead by example and show them how it's done by providing yourself messages of love, excitement, and positivity.

And while the messages we send ourselves are paramount, the messaging we send to others is also very important to consider.

Not only are we constantly sending messages about how we want to be treated, but we are also constantly sending messages of who we are and what our dream is.

If you are launching your dream of being a nutrition expert, but you're constantly posting photos and videos with junk food in the background, you may be confusing your consumers. Maybe that junk food is there for a good reason. Maybe it's your teenager's junk food, or maybe your nutrition expert approach is balance and making room to work junk food into your meal plan. Just remember you only have a few seconds with people's attention. Distraction is a huge problem with us beautiful humans. You don't need to be too concerned that humans are easily distracted, but you do need to focus on the part of that challenge you can handle, and that is making it easier for others to get the right message by making sure the message is clear.

Every week I send out acknowledgements to some of Polka Dot Powerhouse's members who I hear, from other leaders, may need some encouraging words. Sometimes those acknowledgements are for something sad such as an illness or a loved one passing. Sometimes it's for joyous reasons such as hitting a business milestone or helping another Dot sister.

Regardless, every week there are some handwritten notes that go out.

For years, I've been doing this, and the message typically starts the same way. For so long it was, "I just wanted to take a moment to…" I had written that same introduction hundreds of times and then last year, the word "just" started to feel off to me. It started to feel almost as if the note was apologizing for itself or that in some way that word minimized the importance of the note I was sending.

Once I actually thought about it, I found I was using the word "just" a lot—in short videos, in emails, everywhere. "I'm just on today to," "I just wanted to tell you," etc. I hadn't even noticed I was using that word up until that point. It had felt aligned to me and comfortable for so long, but one day, I saw it was out of alignment with who I had become. It felt odd because I no longer felt I needed to justify, minimize, or apologize for my place, whether in a note or anywhere else for that matter.

I knew then that it was time to change the message I was sending myself and others with that one little word. I was no longer feeling like an accidental founder. I was no longer questioning my abilities or my place in the Polka Dot Powerhouse family, and although that had changed for me years before, I had spent years using verbiage that felt weak, doubtful, and timid. When I was a small child, I was so shy that if someone spoke to me, I would cry and hide behind my mom's pant leg. That's not who I choose to be as an adult. It was subtle, but the frequent use of the word "just" no longer felt in alignment. I was sending out mixed messaging.

Maybe you don't think there's anything wrong with including "just" in the intro and that's fine. For me, the message it sent was no longer in alignment with me, and it was time for a change. Now, I intentionally omit that word in intros to handwritten notes. When I take time to handwrite a note, it is intentional and means I'm concentrating solely on them. That's powerful. My chosen words now reflect that. Messaging is everything.

Another example of how powerful messaging can be recently showed up for me. Ever since Polka Dot Powerhouse started, group photos have been taken regularly, typically at some type of special event. During most group photos, someone from the group yells, "Shannon, you should be in the front!" My reply was generally, "No." Polka Dot Powerhouse is a sisterhood with everyone having equal value and importance, and for me, at the time, part of the messaging I was sending was that the leader doesn't necessarily stand in front.

Something interesting happened recently. I was visiting a chapter on the East Coast. It's a wonderful, well-established chapter I have grown close to. I feel comfortable around them. I was on a tour of twelve chapters where I presented a day of learning, and while each day was a little different based on the perspectives and challenges the attendees shared during the event, the main theme and messaging was the same. Since, at any given event, there are usually new members in the audience, I always start with my story and Polka Dot Powerhouse's story. Eventually, telling your own story becomes easy, and you can do it in your sleep, 24/7, on a running loop. I don't even think about it anymore, but sometimes I reveal a new detail or layer that I previously hadn't. I do it without even realizing it, similar to the way it would unfold in a conversation with an old friend.

At this particular event, I was telling the usual story. When I get to the part of my childhood home life, I typically generalize it by saying, "Our family had a lot of secrets." That's what I've said for ten years. But for some reason, at this event, I found myself suddenly giving more details about my life and the difficult relationship I had with my dad growing up. There was nothing too specific and nothing too messy, but there were more details than I had ever shared before. For a few moments, I was mortified. The old familiar "what if they see me" loop started playing in my head. I even lost my focus for a moment and froze. I remember looking at the door and wanting to escape. But as I looked around the room, I realized I was okay. I was in a safe place with people who loved and respected me. They had seen me. They had seen a new part they had never seen before, a raw part I had always tried to hide. No one was leaving the room, no one had given me a look of disapproval. No one was shaking their head in disgust or placing shame on me.

Even though I had tears running down my face and felt sheer terror due to sharing more than I ever had and more than I had intended to, no one was making me pay for it. Some of them were crying with me. Then I saw four members had created the Polka Dot Wall to my right side to demonstrate that they would not let me fall. (An important part of Polka Dot culture is to stand in the back of the room and face the speaker as a sign of respect, appreciation, and love.)

The whole memory is etched in my brain as a wonderfully impactful moment. But that's not all. Later in the day, we had a group photo. Without even thinking about it, something shifted in my normal group photo routine. I went and stood right in the front. It suddenly occurred to me that I was standing front and center.

Normally, upon realizing this, I would have hurried to make my way to the back row, but that time I stood firm and smiled. I was not in the front row because I felt better than anyone else. I was in the front row because I felt equal and worthy to everyone in the group; I felt so much pride to be among them as I stood in the front. I still firmly believe that one of Polka Dot Powerhouse's most beautiful aspects is that all members, including leaders, have equal value and importance. I stood firmly in the middle of the front row that day because I was no longer afraid to be seen. I had told myself that the previous messaging of me standing in the back of group photos supported my belief that everyone has equal importance, but it had also conveniently and secretly shielded me from being seen and therefore kept me safe.

When I was in school, I was one of the first girls to gain height and breasts. I was always thrown in the back as one of the tall ones. As that became my normal spot, I also learned to hunch over to hide my chest. Somehow, that security of being shielded and hidden had carried over into my adult life, and I had never connected the two. I hadn't realized it until the shift during that Polka Dot Powerhouse event that day. In that moment, I no longer felt the need to be shielded. I felt like being seen, standing proudly among my Dot sisters. I was of equal importance and value to my Dot sisters, and I was right up front, willing to let everyone see me. Ever since that monumental day on the East Coast, my messaging has changed, at least somewhat.

I'm fairly tall, so there will still be times I need to stand in the back of a group photo so as not to block people behind me, but I will do so only because of the "tall ones in the back" rule and not because of my internal need to not be seen. Those days are over. My new messaging is that I am thrilled to be here with you, an equal woman who is worthy to call herself a leader. I will stand front and center to let everyone know Polka Dot Powerhouse's leader does not need to hide; rather, she will proudly be seen.

Smiling is yet another area where my messaging has seen a shift. Not everyone knows this, but I went through a lengthy bone grafting journey a few years back. I needed some dental implants done, and due to a prior accident and injury, I did not have the bone density to support them. What followed was a long, expensive, and painful process. Part of that journey involved a procedure where they pulled down my gums, stuffed them with cadaver bone, and sewed them back up with hopes it would grow and provide the bone I needed. This was done right in the front of my mouth—the front three teeth. They removed the implant I previously had there to give that space all the room it needed for the cadaver bone to grow.

To make it appear I had teeth, I wore a clear retainer with little fake teeth in it. If you were to casually talk with me or hear me speak at an event, you likely wouldn't notice it. But I found if I smiled too big, especially while speaking or getting photos done, or if I was very close to someone, they would notice something didn't look quite right. I started feeling self-conscious about it and quickly became an expert at smiling with my mouth closed. Every smile, every barely smile, was with my mouth closed. No matter how happy I was, no matter the situation, my mouth was closed.

The bone grafting was a success—thank goodness—and I now have permanent implants that look beautiful. I've had them for several years now and almost forget the bone grafting journey even happened. Recently, I was traveling, and one of the fabulous Legacy Leaders, Tara, who lives in the area I was traveling in, met me in the hotel lobby to catch up and spend some time together. It was a lovely time. At the end, we decided we wanted to post a photo together. After we took the photo, Tara turned to me and said, "One day, I hope to make you happy enough that you smile with your teeth."

The comment stunned me. I realized that Tara and I hadn't known each other during my bone grafting journey. I started to explain to her why I smiled with my mouth closed, an old habit I hadn't quite let go of yet. I suggested we take another photo, and I smiled a great big, toothy smile. She and I both laughed. Still, back in my hotel room, I continued to process her profound comment. "To make you happy enough that you smile with your teeth." Was I putting out the message of being unhappy or not being present with that closed-mouth smile? If Tara—who I know understands, respects, and accepts me— thinks that, what must a new member or guest who just met me be thinking? I am happy and so grateful to be anywhere I am, and I knew that messaging did not align with how I felt. And while old habits tend to die hard, I now smile with my teeth, another way I'm able to send the message of how grateful and happy I truly am and how I want to experience even more reasons to feel that way.

I hope my stories illustrate how important our messaging to the world is. I want to encourage you to consider what messaging you are sending to yourself and out into the world. To survive launching a dream, you will need to frequently revisit what messaging you're intentionally or unintentionally sending. It is not only important to your audience and the dream you are the keeper of, but also to your own well-being and sanity. I highly recommend writing down the type of messaging you want to send. Writing things down has extra power and helps concrete ideas, thoughts, and concepts into your brain. Write down, in great detail, all the messaging you want to send into the world, and follow that by writing down ways you can send that message.

Anytime someone has the wrong impression of what you were trying to convey, or anytime you feel something is "off," write some more. Write down what message was not received or was sent incorrectly, and see if you can figure out whether that unintentional messaging needs to change. Often, it will be due to the other person's perspective, which is none of your business and out of your control, but sometimes, working it out in writing helps us see where unintentionally confusing messaging is being sent into the world.

Your messaging is you, and since you are the keeper of the dream, your messaging is important to the dream, too. Be truly yourself—you're the only person you can pull off anyway, and that's all you need to be. Make sure you're sending the message you want to send about who that person is. Both you and everyone meant to be impacted by you deserve that type of attention.

An Opportunity for Growth

Everything you do and say is a message not only to yourself, but also to the world and the universe about what you want more of. There is a huge responsibility in that.

A Reason to Celebrate

You are an adult with free will, and you get to decide what message you send to yourself and others.

CONTROL YOUR FOCUS AND DISTRACTION

Learning to control focus is one of the greatest contributors to happiness and success.

Thank goodness for my squirrel brain. It's built perfectly for this journey, but it is still, on occasion, a royal pain in the backside. It sees every sparkly thing. Every. Single. One. And wouldn't you know it, the world is made of sparkly things. Interestingly, there are many reasons to be grateful for all of the lovely distractions in life. Some present as new opportunities, we might catch a glimpse of the competition and what they're doing, and even the people around us and all of their needs and ideas can be beautiful sparkles, too. The world is full of millions of shiny things that are truly wonderful, but are also absolutely not for me. Still, they sparkle, and my mind sees them. Sometimes I think the sparkles test us; they challenge us to see how committed we are to what we're doing, testing us to see our loyalty and commitment to our dreams.

Early on, I realized that if my dream of Polka Dot Powerhouse was going to get anywhere at all, I would need to learn how to focus and to lay down some boundaries and standards to make that focus happen. You see, the world will always continue to sparkle, and that is a wonderful thing, but you and I sometimes forget we get to decide where our attention goes. We aren't intended or obligated to have our attention diverted for every little sparkly thing.

When launching a dream, a large part of your survival as an extraordinary human is going to come down to focus. It is the most important thing you can address and one of the things you can control. Just as everything is either love or fear, everything is also a distraction or something we focus on.

Sometimes we need to be distracted. We were not meant to stay focused forever. We all need that day on the boat with the wind in our hair or a day hunkered under the blankets, binging a good series. On a highly productive day, we all need breaks to refuel, relax, let ourselves chill, and reflect. Whatever healthy distraction looks like for you, just know you need it. I would never say otherwise.

However, you will also face another type of distraction, the one that keeps your dream halted and keeps you feeling bad or frustrated with yourself.

When you're *that* kind of distracted, you find yourself repeating thoughts like, *Why would I keep doing this to myself?*

These distractions are a form of self-sabotage—when we do things or commit to things we know will take away the time, space, or energy we need to work on our dream and that shift us out of our zone of genius (we all do it). You will want to work on becoming aware and addressing these habits as they show up on your journey. When self-sabotaging distractions go unaddressed, they can be the perfect partner for misery and staying stuck while launching a dream. It could even mean the death of your dream.

Whether your favorite flavor of distraction is overcommitting, worrying what everyone thinks of you, comparing yourself to others on social media, relying too much on experts, or the hundreds of other possibilities, just know that distractions can provide a seemingly safe harbor that numbs the reality of needing to take action toward your dream. Everyone has a distracting vice (or many) they choose to stay in partnership with, but as the keeper of a very important dream, it is paramount for you to keep distractions to a minimum. Your dream is too important to risk. While these distractions keep you safe and numb, the real meat of life for a visionary can be found in the deep end of launching a dream, in moving that dream forward, even when it's tempting not to, not only for yourself, but also for those who will be greatly impacted by it.

Choosing to stay in focus is a muscle, and like any other muscle, it takes practice. Once you find yourself being led by an unhealthy distraction (and odds are this unhealthy distraction has shown up before), it is a sign that you need to take action. What action you take will depend on you and your personality. For example, if your unhealthy distraction is over-committing, you might need a written contract with yourself. You may need to limit how often you check emails or return calls, or you may need to designate certain days of the month to reviewing new ideas, etc.

Decide what your chronic, unintended distractions are and then create some boundaries and standards around them to help you stay focused and in your zone of genius longer, so you can help yourself and impact the world as you were intended to do.

An Opportunity for Growth

Unintended distraction is a form of self-sabotage and can keep you from launching and growing your dream.

A Reason to Celebrate

Focus is like any other muscle, and you can grow it to be a rocket to propel you forward.

STOP BEING AFRAID OF THE DARK

You might as well make friends with it.
You're going to be in the dark a lot.

When I was kid, I spent a lot of time in the darkness—the darkness of uncertainty, the darkness of chronic worry, even the literal darkness of the utilities being shut off, again. So much time in the dark. I learned to make friends with it. I learned to find the blessings and gifts hidden within it and the reason I was chosen to spend so much time in it. Since the dark became my normal place to be, I learned almost everything I know about myself and everyone around me by viewing them not only in the shininess of the light, but also in the calmness and clarity of the dark.

While these days I spend much more time in the brilliance of the light because I've learned light is all around us, I still grow and function in the dark as I now know there is nothing to fear there. Challenges keep showing up for me, and they will for you, too. I say that if we're still alive, it means we have more work to do on ourselves (for ourselves and for others, too), and much of that work will be done in the dark.

Sometimes when you're in that deep end, launching and protecting your dream, it's going to be dark.

The darkness can be scary. There's a lucrative film genre built completely around how scary things are in the dark.

But the truth is, living things do most of their growing in the dark; we only see the results of this growth in the light.

Think about every challenge and all the chaos and turmoil you've been through, whether related to your dream or not.

You were forced to grow to get through those tough times, and you did. The darkness is not to be feared. Challenges and chaos will continue to show up for all humans for all time, so even if you cannot quite learn to enjoy the dark, you may want to find a way to at least make peace with it.

Being in the darkness also forces us to focus. Have you ever tried to find a light switch in an unfamiliar room in total darkness? You have to focus to get to the light switch without tripping and flying over furniture. Focus is another gift of being in the middle of challenges and chaos. You have to focus to survive it all.

The darkness also brings clarity. Sometimes, you don't even notice a situation happening around you until you are thrown into the dark of a new challenge. Sometimes, you see something about someone you had never seen before, the truth of who they were or what the relationship truly was, but you don't see it until you're in the dark. And you'll darn sure find out who has your back when things are less than perfect.

My point here is that challenges and chaos happen for all of us—darkness is here to stay, and there is no two ways about it. Even if you do everything to near perfection, you won't be given a pass.

Learn to see the lessons, the blessings, the growth, and the clarity of the dark. You don't always have to enjoy it when it shows up on your doorstep, but unless you like living in misery, you might want to start making friends with it. The dark times are there to help you grow. The times of light are there to show you how the dark was your ally, rather than your enemy, and to help you grow strong enough to enjoy all of your growth and success.

An Opportunity for Growth

The darkness keeps showing up, as we all have work to do as humans. It can be scary and can keep us from moving forward unless we learn to see it for the blessing it is.

A Reason to Celebrate

When you realize what the darkness really is—a way for you to grow and learn—you can make friends with it and use it as a tool.

Survival Tip #8

USE THE "THANK YOU, NO THANK YOU" SANDWICH

Saying "no thank you" to what's not meant for you is simply a way of loving yourself.

Do you come from the good girls' club like I do? It is the place where we were taught to be nice and keep everyone happy. Yep, that's how I learned it, too.

Back when I was young, I somehow accepted the role of making sure everyone was happy and that everyone was okay. As I grew up, I learned that trying to make everyone happy is an impossible job. It's neither my business nor my problem if anyone is happy, except for myself, and I certainly have no control over how others feel. But being too young to understand the impossibility of it, I spent years trying to be perfect at this job I had accepted, and it made me utterly miserable. *Miserable.* There's a lot of pain found in doing the impossible task of making everyone happy, and it never works. Not ever.

Many years ago, I decided I simply couldn't do it anymore. I decided to change. For me, that change was laying down some very firm boundaries and high standards.

Now, you've probably heard it said before that we teach people how to treat us. Well, before I started laying down boundaries, I had taught people that what they could expect from me was a doormat of a person who couldn't say no.

So, when I changed the rules and changed what people could expect of me, I received a lot of pushback. I vividly remember a close relative of mine saying, "You used to be so nice." To whom? I learned then that "nice" means doormat to some. As far as chasing a dream is concerned, being a doormat is the ultimate distraction. No more. Never again. I think of myself as a kind and heart-led person, but some people describe me as the "B word" because I have those standards and boundaries, and I am very clear about them. That's fine. They can believe whatever they like about me. It's not my problem. I know who I am, and I am unapologetic and immensely proud of the woman I have become and the strengths I have developed.

One way I demonstrate my boundaries and standards and help rid myself of needless distraction is by saying no a lot. When someone comes to me with an opportunity, I've gotten really good at figuring out whether it's a "hell yes" or a "hell no." Every once in a while, it's a "hell maybe," which means I need time alone, away from the noise, to clear my head and get clear on what I want.

Whenever the verdict is "hell no," I stick to my guns. It doesn't do me or anyone else any good to take something meant for someone else.

As a founder and the keeper of a very important dream, it's even more imperative that you learn this lesson as early as you can. You're going to come into contact with countless amazing people whose happiness you have no control over but to whom you can certainly contribute if you focus on moving that dream forward.

If saying no sounds difficult for you, think of it this way: Saying no is just saying yes to something else. In fact, when you think about it, you're always saying no to something, and when you say yes to something you know isn't meant for you, you are a thief. You're stealing the opportunity from whomever is meant to have the opportunity. You are also stealing the focus that was meant for your dream and putting it toward this thing that is not for you. In doing so, you are negatively affecting each and every person whose lives were meant to be impacted by your dream. So, you can either disappoint the person who is offering something to you that you know isn't right for you, or you can disappoint the other end, those you're destined to affect. Either way, you will be saying no to someone, so it might as well be in a direction that keeps you sane and happy and contributes toward the impact of your dream.

When you do have to say no to an opportunity, there's no reason to be negative about it. To keep the experience positive for everyone involved, I highly recommend the "thank you, no thank you sandwich."

Here's an example of how it goes:

"Thank you, Jesse, for thinking of me for this opportunity. I will need to decline because [insert your own verbiage here or none at all—you never need to justify your reasons]. I have a contract with myself not to take on any more projects until I release something currently on my plate. But I know you'll find the right person, and I will keep my ear to the ground for who that might be." Thank you, no thank you, thank you. It's very simple, and it's very impactful. It helps people feel what is really going on—that you're not rejecting them but rather, you are taking ownership of your life and your actions. That's a beautiful thing.

An Opportunity for Growth

There will be a lot of requests and opportunities that come your way. Some are meant for you, and some are not, but saying no sometimes feels hard.

A Reason to Celebrate

There is a way to say no that lets people know you are not rejecting them, but rather, you're respecting them and yourself.

DEVELOP A WRITTEN CONTRACT WITH YOURSELF

A contract is about clarity and commitment.
Who better to have one with than yourself?

I used to dread mornings. Through a childhood of chronic stress and many years as an adult feeling I had no control of my life, I learned to wake up stressed. It became a habit for me. I didn't even realize it was happening until about 2013. I used to wake up and shoot out of bed when the alarm went off. My husband, Brian, always described it as though I was being held down by invisible ties that would break free the minute the alarm went off, and I would spring up as soon as I heard the noise. He's a hilarious guy, my husband.

In all seriousness, though, he wasn't far off; this girl had stuff to do. There was always something to prepare for or a fire to be put out somewhere. I would wake up in "closer and fixer mode" the minute the day started, and I didn't stop until I laid my head back down. I thought I was being productive. I thought it was admirable. Looking back, it was none of those things. It didn't occur to me how sick it was until one particular day in 2013.

Although at the magazine we always led with "what would whimsy do" and made sure we always had fun, there was always a pay-to-play. There was plenty of stress in publishing and running a magazine. As a result, I would wake up in stealth mode each day, ready to take care of business.

When we sold the magazine, so I could focus fully on Polka Dot Powerhouse, everything shifted. The day after the magazine officially sold and was no longer mine, I woke up in my normal firefighter state, ready to squash whatever blazes were burning, and I realized there were none. I had woken up ready to be stressed, and there was nothing to be stressed about for the first morning in my life. I was forty-four years old, and it was the first day I remember (even through childhood) not feeling stressed from moment one in the morning. I sat stunned. *Wow, girl, that's really messed up,* I thought to myself.

That was the day I decided that waking up stressed and being addicted to stress was no longer who I was. Of course, cutting it off cold turkey was a pretty hard thing to do. There were many more mornings I woke up ready to be stressed, only to remember there was no reason to be. I set out to develop tools for myself because I never wanted to go back there again. Enter the morning mental priming and my contract with myself.

I am a fan of mental priming—let me tell you why. When you walk out into the world each day, it's important you are clear and reminded of what you want, what you intend to do, and how you want it done. Mental priming is a way to concretely clarify these points into the brain each morning, before the world starts shooting arrows of sparkly things at you. When you do mentally prime, it will be as if you have a superhero shield of protection on you. When you don't mentally prime, you will be a moving target. I learned within the first few years of Polka Dot Powerhouse and through some rough lessons that as a founder and keeper of the dream, the world expected a lot of me, which is a good thing, but it can, at times, be overwhelming. We need to put tools in our mental tool belt that provide support for us to meet our own expectations and allow us to maintain our role as keeper of the dream. For me, one of the most beneficial tools is morning priming, and the star of the show is a written contract with myself.

It's so common for people to have contracts for important things. You are likely in a contract for the mortgage on your home or the place you are renting. If you're in business, you most likely have a contract for your clients. Even when you rent a car for five days, you will sign a contract.

To me, a contract is such a sign of a serious commitment and respect between the parties involved that a written path is chosen for that relationship. A contract is clarity. A contract is power.

Almost every time I visit a chapter or speak for an audience, I ask how many people have a contract with themselves. Usually one or two, maybe three, people will raise their hands. Sometimes it's just me.

We have all these contracts floating around out there, but we don't have a written contract with ourselves. Why? That baffles me.

I'm here to tell you that a written contract with yourself can completely transform your life. It can stop you from over-committing. It can be the place where you begin or continue to increase a life of transparent, firm boundaries and high standards. Putting those two things into a spotlight of importance in your life can completely change those you surround yourself with and the opportunities that come your way. It is such a simple action that creates dramatic results.

A written contract sounds daunting and maybe a bit rigid. It is a practice that won't be right for everyone, but for those keepers of the dreams who choose to try it, it's like a light switch of change being turned on.

A written contract can be part of your morning priming. That's how I use mine. Morning priming is vital because it's important to get your mind clear and focused before you head into the busy world. If you don't get into the right mindset before you start each day, you will be a moving target, and that will make you vulnerable to endless distractions. You are no victim; you are a victor. Victors don't leave their mindsets to chance; they choose what they focus on and who and what they surround themselves with. A great way to maintain that victor mindset is morning priming.

Morning priming can include any number of things. What keeps you grounded yet reminds you of who you are and where you're going? That should be included in your morning priming. There is really no right or wrong way to do it. Make it work for you.

Including a written contract into your morning priming is easy, and I am going to teach you how.

A contract sounds long and detailed, but it doesn't have to be; it can include just one simple principle. What is something you keep finding yourself frustrated with? You can start with that. For many people, that first principle may stem from the fact that many of us overcommit.

Start with one term. Write it down. Read it every morning as you do your morning priming.

Let's say yours is, "I will not accept any new projects until I release or complete a current one." Okay, that's a really good one.

Now, you go out into the world. Someone who heard you're a yes girl comes at you with an "opportunity." This is where the written contract is wonderful. You decline with the "thank you, no thank you" sandwich and also reference the contract. "Thank you for thinking of me, Sally. I need to decline because I have a contract with myself not to take on any new projects until I release a current one, but I appreciate you thinking of me, and I know you will find the right person."

This accomplishes two things. First, it stops you from accepting a self-sabotaging distraction that was meant for someone else, and second, it helps the person being declined to swallow it easier. You aren't rejecting them. You aren't rejecting the opportunity they have offered you. You are simply owning your power and respecting an important agreement you have made with yourself.

I can't control what people say behind my back, but no one has ever said a nasty word when I reference this agreement with myself. They more often come back with, "What's a contract with yourself?"

I know that's not how it always goes. Sometimes they come at you with their great big eyes and mention how much the opportunity, or those involved with it, need you. And you know there are always puppies and orphans involved. How can we say no to puppies and orphans?

Here's the best part. The primary rule of the contract with yourself is that you can only renegotiate when you're alone, ideally during your morning priming. Of course, there will need to be times when you renegotiate your contract with yourself. You're going to change and evolve and so is your dream and its demands, but mindful negotiations can only be made when someone isn't staring you down with big eyes and the aforementioned puppies and orphans.

I've had a contract with myself for about eight years now, and it has grown to be several pages long. I can tell you that it's saved me from so many self-sabotaging tendencies and habits. It has been a great vehicle for getting me out of self-induced trouble before I can get into it.

If this sounds intriguing, and you're curious about it, I highly recommend you try it. Again, start small, and build from there. I think you're absolutely going to love it.

An Opportunity for Growth

The world likes to slobber abundance and the opportunity for it all over us. We can get overwhelmed and lose our clarity if we don't implement ways to support ourselves.

A Reason to Celebrate

There is a way to get mentally clear every morning and stay in alignment, no matter what comes your way.

WRITE A THANK-YOU NOTE TO YOURSELF EVERY SINGLE DAY

Some days you will be the only one thanking you.
You're really going to need that.

Another cornerstone part of my beautiful morning priming is writing a thank you note to myself every day.

Being a keeper of a dream is one of the most rewarding gifts in the world. You and I are so blessed to be doing what we do that impacts not only our lives, but also the lives of so many others. However, we both know it's also really, really hard. If it were easy, everyone would be doing it, but they're not. To the outside world, you're going to make it look really easy. Your social media account is going to show the highlights. You're going to meet people who have been impacted by your dream, and they're going to be so happy to see you and so appreciative of the way you've changed their world. The majority of the time, it's going to be amazing, and you're going to pinch yourself to see whether it is actually a dream.

You're also going to have heavy loads to carry. You're going to be pushed as you never have been before. Important gifts like the one you and I have been given are not given without an immense amount of sacrifice. Don't worry about that now;

you're strong enough to handle it, or you would not have been sent the dream.

That being said, the world is not going to be able to see or relate to how much blood, sweat, and tears you are sacrificing to make your dream happen and to keep it on track. They won't see the sleepless nights, the long hours of endless dedication, or the struggles and mountains you overcame. They aren't meant to be involved in all that. They are simply meant to be impacted by your dream.

There will be so many times your work will feel thankless. No one will see or be grateful for the hard work and sacrifices you are making, nor should they be. They are simply meant to be impacted by your dream. You're going to need someone to rely on for a little acknowledgement on a daily basis. You'll need that like an air tank would be needed to help you stay down in the deep end longer. That one person could and should be you. Who better than you to set the example of the way you want the world to see you and acknowledge you? Most days, it will be you thanking you, and that is enough. The deliberate act of thanking yourself is powerful in so many ways. First, and most importantly, it feels really good. To find something to thank yourself for on a daily basis helps get your mind right and helps you stay focused on where the gold is and on what there is to be grateful for. There is always something. It also sends a very clear message to God or the Universe about what you want more of. You want more ways to feel good, and you want to find more things to be grateful for.

The act of writing the thank-you note is, in and of itself, a very powerful exercise. Thinking grateful and powerful thoughts is wonderful, but I've found, at least for me, that the act of *writing* the thank you note is like cement. It helps my brain grab it better and receive it on a different level. I highly recommend writing it out to level up the effects.

I write a thank-you note to myself every single day, even when I am traveling. There's always an excuse to get us out of the zone, and there is also always a way to make things work, especially the things you are committed to. I carry thank-you notes in my luggage and purse. I never want to be stranded and unable to continue this practice; it has truly changed my life.

Here is how I structure my thank-you note to myself:

1. Find a quiet space. I highly recommend doing this first thing in the morning. It helps prime the brain and get it in gear before the world comes at you with distractions. The act of claiming power and love first thing in the morning sends a strong message of what you want more of during the rest of the day.

2. Grab the thank-you note. Remember, we are always sending messages to ourselves and others. Consider the thank-you note you choose for yourself and what writing utensil you choose to write it with. What message, if any, does it send about how you feel about yourself and what you want more of? If you choose the leftover thank-you notes from your kid's graduation party, that's fine, and the exercise will still have power, but I implore you to consider getting special thank-you notes and a fancy pen for this exercise. It's a way to level up with it and sends a powerful message to you and the world.

3. Make sure you date the thank-you note. That will be important later.

4. Write something you are grateful for. When you first start, it will be great big, grand things. Over time, you'll run out of big things and will need to get more creative. That's okay. A nice reminder in the beginning is to pace yourself. You're going to do this every day.

5. Write something you forgive yourself for. In my opinion, guilt is a wasted emotion. It does no good other than to distract us and kill our momentum. It's a great part of the exercise to simply release yourself, in writing, from something that has been weighing you down. What an exercise in love!

6. Now, write something that gives you fuel—a simple "I love you," "You got this," or, "I believe in you."
7. Sign and seal the thank-you note.

Mine might look something like this:

06/20/22

Dear Shannon,

Thank you for always keeping your line of vision focused. It affects so many people, and I know how hard you work at that.

I forgive you for not taking as much time as you wanted for yourself yesterday. You will make it up another day.

Don't forget that what you do matters and is impacting so many people. Don't give up. You've got this!

Love you,
Shannon

8. Then I seal it in an envelope and keep them all in a box.
9. Here we go with some extra magic. When you're having a really bad day or feel like giving up, sit in a quiet place with your box of thank-you notes. Tear them open, and read through each one. Realize how far you've come and how much you've overcome. This is not the hardest it's been; you've made it through a lot.

Give this a try, and you'll see it is a game changer.

An Opportunity for Growth

There will be so many days no one will thank you, appreciate you, or even acknowledge you.

A Reason to Celebrate

You no longer need to wait for anyone to deliver the love and acknowledgement you seek. You are the person to do it for yourself.

Part Two

THE DREAM

SEE THE DREAM FOR THE GIFT IT IS

This is not a drill. You've been sent something big!

Polka Dot Powerhouse was born out of confusion—a gift in the midst of the chaos in my brain. Tina sent me the name and helped clear things up for me, and for that, I am so grateful. We say every new member of Polka Dot Powerhouse is a sister Tina has sent. Even so, it sure didn't look like a gift when it first came. I found myself, two months after launch, with only one paid member, which left me feeling like an utter failure and Polka Dot Powerhouse looking like just another crash and burn story.

Your gut always knows the truth, and my gut kept whispering and sometimes shouting, "Don't give up! Don't give up!" I could not see through the darkness of ignorance and fear at the time, but my heart and my gut knew better. They knew that what lay ahead was a tremendous gift, even if the world wasn't so sure yet.

You have a dream. It might be a personal dream or a business dream. Some might call it a goal, but I'm going to call it a dream because it's important, but it's a bit bigger than a goal.

This dream of yours is likely a bit of a stalker. It just won't leave you alone. You may have tried to quiet this dream, to ignore it, but it still keeps showing back up in your heart. You may have tried to discard it or to disqualify it or your place in it. Who are you to have this dream? You may not have all the experience you need or that you see others in your industry have. Where do you start? How do you set this dream on fire, so everyone who is meant to be impacted can see it from where they are? That's the big question.

You may have spoken to others about this dream, or maybe you haven't. Whether or not you have spoken it out loud, you likely have people in your life whom you haven't told about this dream, or at least the full vision of it. You must have a good reason for that. Perhaps the people you haven't enlightened may love you fiercely and want the best for you, but you know from past experiences they will either feel the need to try to protect you, or they may even be afraid of what happens if you fail or, worse yet, succeed. You know who I'm talking about. We all have those people, and they are definitely a blessing, which I will talk about later.

My vision, Polka Dot Powerhouse, is, at the time of this writing, ten years old. We are a global community, a family if you will. Polka Dot Powerhouse is way bigger now than I ever dreamed or envisioned it being. It's a darn good thing that I couldn't see how big and impactful it would become. If that had been shown to me when we began—in my naïve and professionally immature stage—I am sure we wouldn't be here today. I would have cut and run, no doubt about it. Knowing up front all the things I would have to know, learn, and experience along the way would have been far too scary. I didn't have the strength or experience to manage my way through all of that when I first started on this journey. It's a really a good thing you're only shown what you need when you launch a dream.

Even if you are whirling in a pool of overwhelm right now, and even if you can't see the way forward or understand how it will all work out, trust.

Trust that you've been sent this dream as a gift for not only you, but also the rest of humanity. Trust this gift is the key to a bigger purpose, and trust that you were sent this gift because you—yes, *you*—are the one to lead it forward into the frontier of opportunity. All dreams that hound you and keep tickling you when you're not looking are a gift. The question is will you be brave enough to open that box and see what's inside for you and the world, or are you going to let the beautifully wrapped gift stay in your heart and mind, unopened and gathering dust?

An Opportunity for Growth

A dream that bugs us and won't leave us alone can be annoying, scary, and stressful.

A Reason to Celebrate

It's all in the way you look at it, and you can shift the focus to see all the ways your dream is an incredible gift.

REMEMBER THERE ARE NO MISTAKES. YOU RECEIVED THIS DREAM FOR A REASON!

There's a great big reason you were sent this dream.

Who was I to have this dream of Polka Dot Powerhouse? As the worst connector in the world, it seemed ridiculous. I truly thought it was a mistake, but it would not leave me alone.

In that car on that fateful day, the day I was bawling my eyes out, the day Tina sent me the name, I knew I had no choice. I knew I had to do this. For my sister, yes, of course. She sent me the name for a reason, but it was also for my gut, which was exhausted from trying to get me to move, constantly assuring me it would not let me down.

I moved forward even though I was sure there was some mistake. I moved forward in fear of being found out.

I can only imagine my gut was rolling its eyes at me. *What do we have to do to convince her that this is right? What's it going to take?*

I'm a bit stingy on trust, and I do not give it easily. So, for me, the fact that I kept moving when everything else said quit was the biggest display of trust I had ever shown.

I now have the confidence to know that Polka Dot Powerhouse is bigger than me and bigger than any one person. The

Polka Dot Powerhouse family and its mission has a beautiful path forward that will continue to impact countless lives. No one knows what's coming in the future, but I can absolutely breathe, now knowing that Polka Dot Powerhouse is where it is supposed to be. I am so thankful to be in this place, but I can still feel the sweat of those years of terror on my back. I know what it is to launch a dream. I know what it is to leap into the deep end and not know what's below.

You may feel the same sometimes. I think most founders and keepers of the dream feel it from time to time. If it were easy, everyone would be doing it.

One thing I can tell you for sure is that if you have a dream, a dream that will not leave you alone, a dream that keeps coming back, you are the one who is meant to start the action on it. Let that sink in. I'll say it again. If you were given this dream, and the dream keeps walking around in your heart, *you* are the person who is meant to take action on it. That's a really big deal, and it can feel pretty scary, but you and I already know that most life-changing things do.

In the early years, I know I certainly felt the dream that had taken up residence in my heart had been sent to the wrong person. So many thoughts of doubts flooded my head.

What if they find out?!? What if they see that the person who owns this global women's connection company is not only the world's worst connector, but also an ambivert (equal parts introvert and extrovert), an ENTJ (commander) personality type, and a Capricorn (driven, ambitious, and hard-nosed) with a very tilted strength set that includes no detail-oriented skills? This is obviously a mistake, right? A leader of a connection company is expected to be the most outgoing, easygoing, and sweetest person on earth, right? What if they find out? What if they see me?!?

For so many years, I was just biding my time, trying to hide under the cover of ignorance and masks, enjoying the ride while it lasted but waiting in sheer terror to be discovered. You know what? That day never came. I sought help and listened to many experts, experts who were well intentioned and very excited but ones who had no idea what the dream needed. I tried to pretend I was something (many things) I wasn't, but I wasn't fooling anyone. Everyone could see right through my cape of pretending, as anyone can when a person tries to be someone other than themselves.

Much to my surprise, no one punished me for it. No one told me my time was up. No one told me to hand the reins to someone better equipped or someone stronger. Instead, what I discovered, over time, was that the more I revealed me—the *real* me—the more people embraced both the dream and me, the stronger my connections became, and the more comfortable I became in my own skin and in the role I was in. I was better able to stand my ground when someone unknowingly tried to pull the dream off track. There were, and still are, many people who don't like me. I'm not ice cream, and my job isn't to please everyone.

What I've learned on this founder journey is that those who were meant to be in your life will be drawn to you like a powerful magnet; there's no keeping them away. Those who were not meant to be in your life at that particular time will not even notice you exist or will feel they dislike you. This is actually good news. If everyone on earth liked you and wanted to spend time with you, you wouldn't even be able to go to the bathroom, much less focus on and launch a fabulous dream.

You can trust in that and in your role in the life of this dream. It was *not* sent to you by mistake. That just doesn't happen. There is something very special in you that this dream needs to be able to begin and survive. You are the oxygen and light it needs to thrive. You are the only one who can do it, or the dream would have been sent to someone else. You are the only one who can take action on this dream. The dream needs *you*!

That's a pretty powerful truth. It may feel scary to hear or say or even think, and that's okay. That's a part of the design of launching a dream—a founder who is scared to death but strong enough to forge ahead into the darkness of the unknown, likely surrounded by those who don't understand or often don't even appreciate the journey. Right now, all you need to remember is that you can trust that if a stubborn, always present dream was sent to you, it is a valuable and rare gift, and it was sent on purpose, *for* a very powerful purpose. Sure, someone may have a similar dream, and maybe they will even launch it, making you feel as though you missed an opportunity. Maybe you did. But they didn't take your dream because your dream, your idea, is exclusive to you. No two dreams are exactly the same because they're being seen through different lenses. Your specific dream was sent to you because you are the only one who sees it through your unique lens, and you are the only one strong enough to keep it in alignment and protect it. It needs you.

An Opportunity for Growth

Sometimes a dream can seem like a mistake. Who are you to have this dream?

A Reason to Celebrate

You were sent this dream because you are the one and only person who is strong enough to take action on it and protect it. The dream is a great big gift, and it needs you.

DEDICATE THREE MONTHS OF FOCUS

You don't need to have it all figured out.
You just need a plan.

I'm not a detail person. Details make me itch. You don't need to console me or feel sorry for me. It's who I am, and it's not a mistake. It's simply not anywhere near my zone of genius. That's okay. It doesn't need to be because I have plenty of other people around me that *are* detail people, and I have the ability to use reverse engineering to get stuff done.

When I talk to most early founders, their main question is "But, *how*? How did you launch Polka Dot Powerhouse? How did you make it a success? How did you this or that?" I know everyone is looking for that shiny magic bullet to success. I can't blame them—I was looking for it in the early days, too. Success leaves clues. Many of us always try to find those success footprints to make our lives easier. Why wouldn't we? It only makes sense.

I can tell you as a visionary with no detail skills that I really struggled. When I say no detail skills, I mean just that. I get overwhelmed by them. I feel nauseous thinking about them. I don't manage them well. I procrastinate addressing them. And let me tell you, you need a lot of detail skills for launching a global connection company or launching any company for that matter. Details aren't my zone of genius—they aren't even in my zone of mediocre. They are in my zone of utter ignorance and confusion.

In the present day, I have surrounded myself with a highly detail-oriented team to balance my slanted strength set. When we started, I didn't know how to do that. I was simply trying to keep going without bringing attention to my fears and shortcomings. I don't know what your strength set is, but I can tell you that no matter what your strengths are, reverse engineering will likely need to become your best friend and a passionate hobby. There are so many details to handle when you launch any dream, and there is so much unknown, especially if you are launching a brand-new idea. Visionaries are really good at knowing the starting point and knowing where they want things to end. It is that middle, unknown part that is a bit murky. It's meant to be. You don't and can't know it all.

In addition, when you start, you are likely not to have the exact team built that you will need to help you with all the parts of launching a dream. You don't need to. Reverse engineering will be your assistant in the beginning. It will become part of your roadmap. Many people have a business plan, and that is a needed and wonderful thing, but reverse engineering will act as a great complement to that and will help you keep on track with it all.

When someone winds up cornering me with a big bunch of "but hows," I usually say, "Simply focus on the next step forward, and after that, take a breath and take the next step forward." What is the next step forward? Only you know that answer. You may say you don't know, but the answer is in your gut. It always is. You don't have to know the whole path; you simply need to know the next step.

The first thing to do is to decide what you want the end goal to be. Don't worry; it will look different by the end—it always does. But it's not going to benefit you to focus on that. Where do you currently see this dream of yours landing in the end?

I do, of course, have longer-term goals, but I typically use intense focus for three months at a time with reverse engineering. Here's how that looks. First, based on your long-term goal, decide where you should be three months from now. Make specific goals around that three-month mark, and be as detailed as possible. Then, reverse from there. Based on the three-month goal, what needs to happen two months from now? What needs to happen a month from now? What needs to happen a week from now? You can continue this pattern until you have your goals broken down into daily, or even hourly, goals and action steps.

Write down all the things. Write down all of the action and sub-actions that will be needed for you to hit the three-month goals. Who will you need to talk to? What homework and research will you need to do? What calls will you need to make? What commitments or decisions need to be made and when? Document all of it. Create a path for all of it. Don't just plan, and don't just wish for it. Don't just stare at it and hope the fairies magically bring it. Schedule each and every tiny thing that needs to happen in your plan. Again, don't get too hung up on whether it will look like what you started with at the beginning of the three months. Our goals and paths are always changing and evolving, and that's why we're only starting out by being laser focused for three months at a time. Dedicating three months of intense focus at a time, reversing the steps and needs, and scheduling and taking action on those steps will help you stay motivated, focused, and passionate.

Three months is a nice timeframe of concentration to work on. It's not long enough to overwhelm, yet it's long enough to truly cover some impactful ground. Three months is a sweet spot for focus. Beware because more than three months of focus can feel like a hot mess. For me and other founders I know, three months of focus is the perfect chunk to move the needle.

Most people quit or fail because they think their brains should be good enough to keep them accountable, and they try to focus on large chunks of time. Your brain is an amazing miracle and as smart as it gets. It is a literal computer that will find a way to help you achieve what you want, but it is also a frat house of chaos. Negative self-talk, overthinking about what your neighbor said a week ago, processing all the ideas, planning the vacation—your brain is in charge of all the things. My dear friend and beautiful Dot sister, Nicole Lewis Keeber, describes it as the home of the "itty bitty shitty committee." There's a lot going on in there. To expect your brain to also be the sheriff of holding you accountable for all the micro goals and all the dates and times involved with that is to live in a fairytale. Good luck with all that. No, seriously. Don't set yourself up for failure and distraction from the beginning. You're going to need something more than your beautiful and wonderful brain.

Get yourself a strategic planner, and put those action items and micro items on the books as if they were very important and game-changing appointments because they are. Set deadlines for the implementation of each action step. Book and hold a time for them to be achieved. Dedicate to three months of intense focus to accomplish the actions of your micro goals, and after three months of really giving it your all, reevaluate the next steps on a regular basis.

Reevaluating does not mean simply pushing out new shiny products from the excuse factory. We all have the same twenty-four hours in a day, and we all deal with something going sideways in some part of our lives. How much do you want it? Valid reasons you didn't do your action steps (excuses) will always be available for you in long looping lists. Part of being a human means you will always and forever be cleaning up something. All of us are. Excuses make it easy for us to stay stuck and safe, but they do absolutely nothing at all toward launching a dream. This dream is worth you going the extra mile, inserting an exhilarating level of dedication, and moving beyond the self-sabotaging distraction of inserting a juicy excuse.

By dedicating three months of focus at a time, you're going to see your dream take new paths you didn't even see coming. It may look much different than when it started. That is absolutely normal. Don't get too hung up on that; it can become a damaging form of distraction. Just know the dream will change organically, and sometimes by design, over time.

The goal of three months of focus is not to keep the dream a pristine image of its birth, but it's to help aid in the control of your ideas and thoughts and to make sure primary goals and objectives are being achieved in the huge waves of the dream. Many visionaries are pretty rigid about the vision of their dreams, allowing for short-term laser focus, but hopefully, they're also green enough to allow the flexibility for the dream to go where it's meant to go. If you're not feeling you have the strength to laser focus on anything yet, don't worry. Just keep moving, and make the movements an important priority. Being consistent with those two habits will spark new muscles and skills in you that you never dreamed you could have.

An Opportunity for Growth

While it's good to have goals for different time periods, three months of focus helps you narrow your target, so you can cover more ground on your dream's future.

A Reason to Celebrate

Trying to plan too far ahead can be overwhelming and chaotic, killing your desire to keep the dream going.

EMBRACE THE GIFT OF 300 FEET

Trust me. If you could see any farther, you would run.

Most visionaries, myself included, want to know, from A to Z, how everything is going to work. Women are especially good at this. That strong visionary in us has a plan, and Lord help anyone or anything that tries to get in the way of that. Isn't that the way it is? Only it isn't because it never goes that way. Never.

There's a funny graphic I often see on social media that shows what people think success looks like (a straight line) and what it actually is (a very unstable line with sharp turns, big loops, and bottom outs). The messy path is much more accurate.

When we started Polka Dot Powerhouse, I didn't know where it would go. While I certainly had hopes and crazy dreams, I was simply trying not to drown. I now recognize what a gift it was not to know what was coming and not to be able to see what I would need to know, do, and learn. It would have overwhelmed me so much that I would have never started. Nope. My sweet li'l brain would have said, "I'm not ready, and that sounds like no fun at all." Back then, I was nowhere near ready for all that I am now, and I am not ready now for what is to come in the next ten years, but I can tell you what I do know. The gift of 300 feet assures me that at the exact point I need to be ready, I will have the strength, knowledge, and experience to handle whatever comes my way. It will not be given to me a moment too soon or a second too late; rather, I'll receive what I need at the perfect time I am able to handle it.

I once read that 300 feet is the approximate distance of headlights. There's just enough light to keep you going. Once you're beyond that place, the headlights reveal 300 more feet, and so on.

If you have any amount of experience trying to launch a dream, you likely already know the gift of 300 feet is one of the greatest gifts you can receive. It can feel like a curse, that short distance of sight, but it is a miraculous present wrapped in a sparkly box with a perfect bow. It is there to *help you!* I hope you'll consider starting to see it that way. It is like a firm hand on your shoulder saying, "I trust you with the treasure of this dream, but I respect and love you enough not to overwhelm you in such a way that you completely take off running in the opposite direction."

I can tell you that when we first started Polka Dot Power-house, if someone would have told me I would have to know Canadian laws, have a communications team, or even that we would spread all over the globe, I never would have been able to keep going. Are you kidding me?!? I would have been too afraid, too overwhelmed, and too doubting of my capabilities. I would have run as far away as I could.

We all know that the fewer things we focus on, the better job we can do. While it's good to have a forecasted plan and strategy, you simply cannot worry about every detail of the future. When you're worried about all of the things that are supposed to happen far into in the future, you're not able to devote your focus on doing a good job in the current moment. Something suffers.

Not only that, but you will not be able to be fully present to see and appreciate all that is happening. You may say, "Maybe I don't want to be present in this moment. This moment is really hard, and I want to move on from the mess this feels like and then I can enjoy the ride." You'll have plenty of moments that feel this way. I know most founders feel that way very often. But trust me, when it's one or two years down the line, you'll want to look back on the messes.

You'll look back on them with appreciation of what those situations taught you and led you to. It will be necessary to look back on them from a personal level to see how much you've grown as a leader and a person, along with all you survived. Could new founder Shannon have handled what ten-year founder Shannon is currently handling? No way! Not a chance! There is a perfectly and strategically sound reason new founder Shannon did not get all the info at the beginning—because she simply could not have handled it. Not only that, but things almost never go the way we plan or expect them to. I always say God has a sense of humor.

Each challenge you come upon will build a new muscle in you that will prepare you for a future challenge or opportunity. You don't have to worry about that or be ready for that right now. You can trust that when an opportunity or obstacle comes, you will have the knowledge, muscles, and experience to handle it if it's meant for you. One day, one quarter, one year at a time—300 feet.

Trust yourself and your dream enough to know nothing is moving out of time, and you will be shown what you need to see at the exact moment you were meant to see it, and you'll have the strength and wisdom to see and handle it. Not one second before and not a breath after. At the exact moment. That's an amazing gift. That is the incredible gift of 300 feet.

An Opportunity for Growth

You will have all the tools you need at the exact time you need them. Trust the gift of 300 feet.

A Reason to Celebrate

You don't yet have the strength, wisdom, and experience you will need to keep your dream going beyond the next 300 feet.

KEEP THE DREAM ON TRACK

Oh, the world is full of shiny things. One of the jobs of the visionary is to keep the train on the tracks.

There is a very important reason the dream you have was sent to you and has been following your heart around. Maybe the most important reason is because you will be the key person to make sure the alignment of that vision remains intact and on track.

As your dream impacts more and more of the countless people it's meant to impact, you'll start to notice something— everyone is going to come to the table with their own excitement and interpretation of what the dream is and what the vision of that dream looks like and means. They see it through their eyes and their experiences. Their interpretations of the vision may not be, and usually isn't, the same as yours.

All of these people with all of their interpretations of your vision—your dream—may show up and want to help you. That's great! More help is always needed, right? Yes, but be aware that sometimes the people who want to help will also want to change the dream, sometimes with helpful tiny tweaks and sometimes in great big, broad strokes. This may be intentional or not, but it will be there all the same. This can be both good and bad news, depending on how closely aligned their interpretation is to your actual vision.

Let's take sisterhood for example. The vision of Polka Dot Powerhouse is very simple: to connect extraordinary women across the globe for sisterhood. The end. It's simple, but it's so impactful. Very early on, I realized if you ask one hundred different people what sisterhood means, you are very likely to get one hundred different answers. It's not so simple then, is it? For some people, sisterhood means connections, to others it means education, for some it is pushing against policies, and others it means sharing hobbies. Some have bad anchors to the word sisterhood; they don't like the word at all. For them to get on board, they would want to change it from sisterhood altogether. It is neither right nor wrong—it is what it is when you work with humans who have their own experiences, anchors, feelings, and thoughts. In actuality, it's a really good thing, as long as the founder of the dream (that's you) gets the lay of the land and has a strong enough backbone to stand their ground. That's one of the reasons you were chosen—because you're strong enough to protect this vision, this dream. You may not even feel strong enough yet, but rest assured, there are no mistakes. Whether you are currently strong enough, or the muscles you need to get you there are hiding, you will have them right when you need them.

When I first started Polka Dot Powerhouse, we were small, with roughly thirty members at the end of the first year. It was intimate, cozy, and safe. That suited the desire of many of the members at the time. When we started to take off and had a couple of explosive years of membership growth, some of those members were no longer happy. I didn't see that coming. I thought more connections were better. But for some of the early members, what drew them to us was that tight-knit feeling. I started hearing comments like, "I liked it when it was small," or, "I can't connect with that many members." A few members said they would leave if we got any bigger. So, within our first few years, I was faced with a big decision: should we stop growing and keep it small? I didn't want to disappoint our members, but I could tell from the immense response we were receiving from women all over the world that they needed a community like this. I sat on it for a while. I found real clarity on what our mission is and where I saw it going. I prayed and asked my sister what she thought and then I became quiet. I listened to my gut. I knew exactly what we had to do. I was both excited and grateful for clarity and the prospect of our future, but I was also sad because I knew I would disappoint and likely lose some members. Our mission is to spread sisterhood to the millions of women who need it, so we kept growing and staying open to new opportunities to expand. Did I make some members mad, and did they leave? Yes. Was I disappointed with that? Yes and no. Of course, I never want to disappoint anyone, but it's simply impossible to please everyone. It just doesn't happen. I think, in the earlier years, it was harder for me to accept that. Being a new, inexperienced, and unlikely founder, mixed with the fact that I grew up as a people pleaser, hit me doubly hard and caused a heavy load of guilt over the thought of disappointing people. But I've since learned guilt is a wasted emotion that does not benefit anyone.

Several years in, it became obvious to me that to keep the vision on track, I would inevitably disappoint some. I learned that if you don't stand your ground and keep that vision on track, you will not only disappoint yourself in the long run, but also the countless number of people who were supposed to be impacted by your dream. That's a *lot* of people. You're never going to not disappoint someone; it's part of the pay-to-play. The decision you'll have to make is for what reason you're willing to disappoint others. To keep the dream on track and to be strong enough for it to benefit all the people it's supposed to benefit is a darn good reason in my opinion.

It's not that you won't appreciate and respect those who leave—very much the contrary. The people you will disappoint and who may leave you as a client or customer are very important and were with you the perfect amount of time. Nothing is moving out of time. If they hadn't been there when they were, you may not have grown in experience, muscles, and knowledge. Remember, even when you have to disappoint someone by standing your ground, thank them, wish them well, be grateful for them, and give thanks for them in your quiet time. They are a gift, and so is the fact you held the ground for your dream. Sometimes, you'll even find them returning later in some capacity or another. You have a lot to be thankful for.

Rest assured, all those who start, grow, and protect a vision deal with this. You are not alone. I believe there is comfort in knowing that. It's something that's not talked about nearly enough, but we *all* go through it.

One thing to carry with you always is the realization that being gifted a dream and being strong enough to take action on it is a pretty big responsibility. It means the countless people who are meant to be impacted by your dream are counting on you to do the fun and festive things but, maybe more importantly, also the hard and challenging things. Not only is all of this a huge responsibility, but it's also one of the most rewarding experiences you will ever have, as long as you stay focused on your role and keep moving forward.

An Opportunity for Growth

You will encounter many well-intentioned people on your journey who will unintentionally try to pull the dream off the tracks.

A Reason to Celebrate

You are the keeper of the dream because you are strong enough to keep it on the tracks.

CREATE A FUNNEL OF VISION

In addition to a really clear mission, you're also going to want to know how you want things done.

We've talked about you being the keeper of the vision and the fact that you're going to disappoint some people. That's all part of the process. When I mention these things to entrepreneurs, their next comment is, "But how will I know? How will I know what to bend to and what to stand tall against?" That's a great question. Most founders spend their entire careers working on and tweaking solutions to this very dilemma. No one can give you the exact answer for that except you. Rest assured, while you may not feel like you know right now, the answer is already inside of you. Your gut already knows.

I always say being an entrepreneur is like riding the tight rope between sheer terror and total exhilaration. One critical comment, email, or phone call can throw you into terror, and on the flip side, one note from a customer who has been positively impacted or one record-breaking sales day can send you the other direction into exhilaration. You may even feel as though you're getting some mental and emotional whiplash throughout this process. Some days you'll think, I *didn't sign up for this*, or, *I don't get paid enough for this*. Other days, usually just in the nick of time, you'll be reminded of the importance of what you do and catch a glimpse of how your ripple of impact is spreading and helping the planet, and it will all make sense again. This is all by design.

It can feel as if you're riding in a car as a passenger, with your dream behind the wheel, and it's either hitting the gas or slamming on the brakes. You know what I mean. We've all been a passenger in a car with a driver like that, and it leaves you worn out and nauseated all day long.

You will certainly have days when this is the case; we all do—many founders take that nauseating ride every day. I know I did, and it's truly a miserable place to live. The majority of humans simply cannot live that way forever, no matter how passionate they are about their dreams. Eventually, something has to give. The two choices people have are either to scrap it all, get out of the car, and quit, or allow themselves to become miserable enough to make a huge change and get in the driver's seat, choosing a much smoother ride.

I chose to make the huge change and get in the driver's seat, and let me tell you, it all starts and ends with boundaries and standards.

Polka Dot Powerhouse has always made it possible to surround myself with extraordinary humans, truly supportive, giving, and encouraging changemakers. There is truly no feeling like it. It is such a life-altering community that has changed my life, and I am so thankful to be a part of it. However, as every founder and company will likely experience, there is still the need to deal with people on the back end.

Throughout the years, we'd occasionally have someone come through on an administrative or leadership level, and at first, all would be well. We would enjoy working together, and the dream and all the scenery was amazing... until I would say no. When I would say no, they would be mad, leave, or pull the "I thought this was a sisterhood" card, as if sisterhood was code for "you owe me." It was rare this would happen, but it always shook me a little. In our early years, and with me being so inexperienced, I would always take it like a sucker punch.

The people-pleasing little girl in me would feel as if she had let the world down. After the initial wound healed, I would always ask what I should learn from it and how I could avoid that type of thing in the future.

What has worked best for me in the long run is being a badass about standards and boundaries and being absolutely unmovable about Polka Dot Powerhouse's mission. *Unmovable*. We always say we're flexible on details but stubborn on vision. That's a fun way to say, "We're not moving unless we want to move!" The truth is the world is full of shiny things—beautiful, brilliant, and sparkly things. Things other companies are doing and things someone *should* be doing. Things others think you should be doing through their lens of what the vision means to them. So many distracting things. The list is endless. It's not a bad thing to entertain these options until it starts to pull you away from your mission. There are so many wonderful things your company could undertake and evolve into, and that's wonderful. From where I sit, the more things you do that do not align with your vision (regardless of how worthy they are), the less you will be able to impact the world in the way and at the level you are meant to. It's simple. Thank you, no thank you, thank you. It's not easy to say no, but it's simple.

My recommendation, whether you're just starting out or have been going a long time, is find real clarity with what your mission is. A mission statement works well. Be as focused and as specific as you can about what your dream's mission is. Once you've done that, write down what you will and will not tolerate from those with whom you are lucky enough to work and those you are honored to have as clients. Do not be afraid to set boundaries and standards for yourself or your work environment with those who work with you and with the expectations you set with your clients and customers. Certainly, some people will be put off by it; they may even say you're difficult to work with. They may even decline to work with you. That's fine. Remember that everyone is seeing your dream and mission through their lenses, not yours. If you are as clear as you can be about your mission, standards, and boundaries, and someone feels they need to leave, let them. It's for their sake and yours, too. If anyone still feels they need to decline once I have been clear with our mission, my work expectations, and what we provide to our members, I think they absolutely need to do it—there's nothing more I can do at that point to make them stay. You either get clear in the beginning and lose a few people, or you deal with some drama when the fog of uncertainly clears. It's a loss either way, but to get it done on the front end will help to eliminate the drama and save both parties time, energy, and wasted effort.

In order to help streamline this process and ensure you're clear, you'll need to create some type of filter to help you stay firm. I call mine "the funnel." Whenever someone comes to me with an idea, it's either a hell yes or a hell no. After ten years, I usually know, without hesitation, what will and will not fit through the funnel. Sometimes I'm not sure, and I have to manually put it through the filter of boundaries, standards, and our mission. The funnel has saved me more times than I can count. I highly recommend it.

In addition to being clear on the mission, you also have to be very clear, as the keeper of the dream, what your vision is for that mission and for those involved. It will certainly evolve and change over time, but it's important to have a handle on the vision at any given moment, so you can more effectively put it through the filter.

Scenarios will arise when something will fit through the filter on mission, but not on vision. For example, in the early days of Polka Dot Powerhouse, certain members wanted us to offer a series of educational classes to our regular members (we've always had an educational component in our Diamond level membership). Sounds nice, right? Yeah, it did to me, too. Other companies in the same industry were doing it, and it sounded as though it might be a natural progression for us. At that point, I put it through our mission filter, and it fit. It would help to connect women, so we proceeded. We tried several different times and in several different ways to make it happen, but we just couldn't find our groove.

Sometimes, when something isn't working, it means you simply need to keep trying from different angles and not give up. But with my scenario, my gut was trying to tell me something. I would feel a pause and a weird, uncomfortable feeling in my gut every time it came up. Eventually, I became so tired of it that we abandoned the idea altogether. It wasn't until years later, when I started to put things through both our mission filter and a newly founded vision filter, that I discovered why it hadn't worked and why my gut had been trying to send me signals.

When I went back and put that idea through the vision filter, I discovered that the distraction of focus it would require for us to have successfully made the educational component work would have hurt our foundational elements. What's even more powerful is that my vision filter involves simplicity and purity of connections. When we didn't try to be an educational facility and stuck to our simple but impactful mission of connecting women for sisterhood, it allowed us to focus all of our energy on the basics while encouraging our members to connect to each other for different educational opportunities they may have needed. This brought us right back to connecting members, which is the purest form of our mission.

It's amazing how a secondary vision filter to complement the mission filter helped to clear up a lot of murky grey area. A vision statement or filter supports the mission statement but with further specifics as to how and through what avenues and opportunities. A mission statement provides clarity around what impact you want to provide the world. A vision statement says in what way the mission will be done, the standards you will hold to get you there, and the boundaries you will adhere to along the path of the dream of impacting people. It's a matter of being as clear as possible, so there is less grey area to confuse or distract you and those helping you. Clarity is power. Although both your mission and vision statements (or philosophies) may evolve over time, finding clarity on them right now and reassessing the level of clarity at any given moment during the journey will save you time and time again and will help you make less mistakes in the future.

An Opportunity for Growth

You will be pushed and pulled and tested until you lay down some boundaries and standards.

A Reason to Celebrate

You are a founder and a keeper of a dream, and there is no one better equipped than you to set the vision for the mission.

DON'T LET MOSS GROW UNDER YOUR MOMENTUM

Just when you get rolling, you're going to want to stop.

I can tell you how it's going to be. You're going to launch this dream (yes, you are), and things are going to get really crazy. That's how it was for me. We launched Polka Dot Powerhouse in 2012. As previously mentioned, it looked like a failure at first, and it took a minute or two for us to find our feet, but by 2014, we were flying high. Abundance was slobbering all over us. That was still back in the early days before I found my confidence and true place and purpose in the company. Much of my attention was still in "let's try to hide" mode and in keeping myself seen but not too seen.

That year, we had about twenty or more chapters launch across the country. It was bananas! When I wasn't traveling (which I was a lot of the time), I was grasping at any amount of family time I could. I felt a mixture of excitement, happiness, overwhelm, and being drowned.

That space was so abundant that there left little time for anything else—no time for strategy and no time for development. Nothing. Travel, speak, eat, sleep, some time with family, repeat. That was my life, and I felt so lucky and overjoyed to be doing it. But in my happily overwhelmed state, I made a big mistake; I let moss grow under my momentum.

I had built Polka Dot Powerhouse and its system and visions for a maximum of three chapters. When we became really abundant, really quickly, it did not occur to me that anything needed to be fixed. We were launching everywhere. Wasn't that proof nothing was broken? Nope!

While I was trying to keep up, the structure started crumbling. Our systems needed to be rebuilt, and our mission needed to be adjusted from one hundred people (where we were at the time) to one thousand (the number we hit in 2015).

It was a really good lesson about what it looks like to become so mesmerized by the smell of a new car that we forget to change its oil and fill its tank.

Learn from my mistakes, and make sure you know that once your dream really takes off, you're going to need to be careful not to forget your dream is always evolving and changing. It will need new systems and approaches as it grows.

Always make sure you schedule time for the maintenance of your dream before you schedule joyrides. For us, that meant we needed to schedule meetings and times for all the necessary components of the business before we scheduled travel, speaking engagements, and fun.

It is a lesson I will never forget. Luckily, our team has grown enough now that those things are always working, and time is being spent on them, whether or not I am traveling and booked solid.

What you and your team (if you have one) are tackling now will show up in about three months. What you are not addressing right now will also show up in three months. If there are vital logistical parts of your dream and its ability to grow and thrive, guess where things will wind up in three months if those parts are not tended to? That's right—on fire. And not in a good way.

I wish someone would have told me, back when we first started and our team was only a few people big, that you schedule the needs first and the shine after. It would have saved me a lot of time, energy, and frustration. So, now I am sharing that lesson with you. Don't let moss grow under your momentum.

An Opportunity for Growth

You're going to be a huge success, and abundance is going to slobber all over you. The tendency will then be to stop and watch the success for a long time.

A Reason to Celebrate

When the dream starts flying, it will be so big and beautiful that it will need your attention. It will never stop needing you.

Part Three

YOUR DREAM AND OTHER PEOPLE

REALIZE YOU CAN'T DO IT ALONE

Oh, you're the whole package, alright, but you were never meant to do it alone.

So, now you're walking around strutting your stuff because you realize how important, powerful, and trusted you are to receive the gift of the dream. That's right! You are the visionary and protector, but you're going to need many other people. You will not be able to and were never mean to do it alone. For most people, that's the hardest part.

When they hear they aren't the complete package to be able to take the dream to completion by themselves, they freeze. They feel as though they're flawed in some way. Then they become distracted by feeling they need to "fix" themselves, so they can deliver to everyone watching them. This is absolutely not true and is completely ridiculous. We can never be good at all the things we need to be, and trying to be that distracts us from our zone of genius. As much the dream needs you, it needs other people, too. If you were meant to do it alone, you wouldn't need anyone else, but you are surrounded by millions of people. There's a reason for that. A lot of people burn out or run out of fuel because they try to do it all themselves. They hear the dream has been sent to them on purpose, and their ego shouts out some nonsense like, "Then you must be all the things it needs." That's a load of crap. No one ever said that. It was invented by your brain. It's never going to happen like that, so save yourself the time and energy of being sucked into that distraction.

I'm pretty protective of myself and my vision. Some of that has to do with Tina sending me the name and, what I believe, the idea was. I owe it to my sister, and all the sisters she has sent me, not to drop the ball. That also means I am very selective about who I work with and what tasks I give them. With me, trust to go deeper into the guts of the mission is earned and gifted. It's that important. I fully embrace that I can't do it alone—that would never work for a connection company, or any other company for that matter. That doesn't mean I don't have expectations, standards, and boundaries. I am known for them.

I have always been so passionate about the Polka Dot Powerhouse vision that I was easily able to get other people excited about it, too. Getting people excited about an idea is one of my top strengths, and let me tell you, I know how to get it done. You will also have many people excited about your dream who want to help. While it is a wonderful thing to have so many people excited about a dream that means so much to you, not everyone is aligned to help you build it or lead it.

Yes, everyone will have a place in connection with your dream. Some will be impacted by it as a customer or client, some will be impacted by you pushing your industry's standards, and a very select group will have a hand in growing it. Not all people will have a place in every category. We will discuss people in more detail later. For now, remember that other people are supposed to be a part of the equation. Decide what you expect from those you want involved *before* you bring anyone on board.

Write down your expectations. While you're at it, write down qualities of the type of person you want to work with and possibly have on your team. There is power in writing things down. Then, watch closely and listen. Those people will show up, maybe even at the very moment you have given up the search. Set the intention, and trust the process; if you are meant to work with them, they will show up, even if in the most unlikely ways.

An Opportunity for Growth

You are exactly who you are supposed to be as the keeper of the dream, but you cannot and were not meant to do it alone.

A Reason to Celebrate

You will have the opportunity to include many people in the building and growth of your dream.

UNDERSTAND THAT WE ALL NEED MORE BRICKS

Everyone you meet has something for you. Pay attention.

I am not only an idea visionary, but I also rely on visuals to learn things. If you want me to get behind an idea, give me a fun or interesting visual to grab onto, and I'll be right there with you.

A great visual I like to use is that your path ahead is a brick road (and it can be whatever color you like). To keep moving forward, you will be in a constant state of needing bricks for your road. Sometimes, when you start spinning, it means you have a gap in the path, and until you receive the next brick, you won't go anywhere.

I believe everyone you ever come into contact with will have a brick for you. It may be a brick of inspiration or motivation, or maybe a brick of understanding. Some of the bricks will simply be for acknowledgement and the wonderful feeling of being seen, while others might connect you to the next person you need. You may not even know what the brick is right away; the reason you were meant to meet or interact with any given person in front of you may not immediately be clear, but

I assure you that reason is there. It may even be as small as a simple smile.

I've met so many extraordinary people on my journey so far, and I believe every single one of them has contributed to me becoming not only who I am as a human being, but also who I am as a leader and keeper of the dream.

The bricks I've received along my journey have provided strength, wisdom, fun, and beauty.

The push is that you can either use these extraordinary bricks to build the path to where you want to go, or you can use them to build a wall to guard yourself, to shelter yourself, and sometimes to self-sabotage yourself and send your dream up in flames. As always, and as it is with everything in life, you have a choice. You get to choose how to use the bricks every contact will give you. Whatever you decide to do with the bricks given to you is your business. Just know, from my experience, if you choose to use the bricks to build a wall instead of a path ahead, you will go absolutely nowhere and neither will your dream.

Let me tell you, the biggest growth for opportunity when it comes to launching a dream is working with people. I absolutely love people, but I'll admit it sometimes takes greater effort to try to figure them out—a wonderful opportunity, if you will. It is the gift that gives and keeps on giving. So many people, both similar to and different from us, are placed in our path. They are there to grow us and help us learn (if they don't drive us insane first). Even for those whose job it is to work with people every day, as is the case with me, it is still a struggle sometimes. It's neither good nor bad. It is what it is and what it takes to be a human.

As with so many other humans out there, I have abandonment issues. My childhood and the experiences I went through grew me into the person I am now, but they also taught me about walls—how to build 'em, tall and strong. When it comes to building a wall, I'm a gifted artist. Being a wall builder is a survival mechanism I learned about at a young age and perfected by the time I was an adult. There's no need to feel sorry for me; it was my normal. I learned to keep people at arm's length for fear they would get too close. That's what I grew up believing.

Other times, I am a naked target, too trusting and seeing only what I want to see. A member of our team always says, "She's got those rose gold-colored glasses on." Yep, that's me, too. Don't try to figure me out; I'm still trying to figure myself out.

The bottom line is we have an endless list of justifiable reasons to keep ourselves and others at a distance, to use the bricks for a wall, one that is tall and strong. However, that not only shields us, but it also hides from us the light of beauty and the view of opportunities. It took me so many years to figure this out, but using the bricks for a path forward brings so much more to life. It can certainly be scary to build an extraordinary path ahead, but the beauty of it will blow your mind.

Anytime you meet with someone, watch for their brick. Keep your heart and mind open to why you were meant to connect or interact with them. There is beauty and hope in understanding that everything is for a reason, and every person is valuable and brought into your path on purpose.

An Opportunity for Growth

You need bricks of connection for your path forward.

A Reason to Celebrate

Everyone has a brick of impact that is meant for you.

IT ONLY TAKES ONE

You don't need a long line of supporters; sometimes it takes only one to light the spark.

When we launched Polka Dot Powerhouse, we had over one hundred people say they were going to join on launch day. I was sweating buckets because the crappy website I had built was never meant to support a high volume of traffic. I was scared to death we were going to crash it. I was stressed beyond measure leading up to launch day. However, when launch day came, we only had one person join, and her name was Cora. She had joined to support me and didn't log back in for a long time. Cora didn't know she was the only paying member, and I certainly wasn't going to tell her. Hell no!

She didn't know it, but with her simple act of signing up, she brought the spark that started the whole thing. The truth is that if Cora hadn't shown up, we likely would have quietly called off the whole thing. We would have put our tails between our legs and hoped everyone would forget it had ever happened. But Cora, she made that impossible for me. Even though I knew Cora had joined and not logged back in, and even though I knew she wasn't using her membership at that time, I felt I owed her. I owed her for showing up. Part of it was that my money-guy husband wasn't going to be keen on a refund being issued, but it was mostly trying to honor and respect Cora and the promise I had made to her when she signed up for a membership. Thank goodness she showed up at the exact right moment! I owe her—Cora, the fire starter.

If you have a dream chasing you around, you don't necessarily need a long line of supporters to keep pursuing it. You only need one person to be onboard and to believe in your dream. That person might be you. You need one spark of belief, along with the action behind that spark. Even though it may be only one spark, it has the potential to ignite a huge flame. Polka Dot Powerhouse is the reluctant poster child of no one quite understanding or believing in it, yet that doesn't mean a darn thing as far as potential success is concerned. If you have one person who is behind you or beside you, you can do miraculous things that will affect countless numbers of people.

There will certainly be times you *do* actually need to throw in the towel, call it quits, or change direction. I'm not discounting that. But let me tell you one thing—the dreamer's gut will always know. Listening to input from others is recommended and helpful, but at the end of the day, the dream was sent to you because you are the only one who can know for sure where it should go. Consider your gut and its knowledge as your most valuable team member. It is. Listen to others, but also get quiet, put those opinions through the filter, and listen to what your gut has to say. It always knows what to do. Always.

I remember how it felt when we had Cora as our sole paying member, and the whole thing felt like a terrible mess. I remember how embarrassed I was, how humiliated. But my gut kept whispering (and sometimes screamed), "Don't quit." It was hard to explain to anyone else on the project why I was choosing to continue on in the face of utter defeat. To them, me having a whisper from my gut seemed to be a pretty questionable reason to continue. I truly think they thought me wanting to continue was about my ego, and maybe a small part of it was. I am a visionary with a history of a lot of ideas. Some were great ones, and others were crash-and-burn scenarios we quickly discarded. Other people wondered (sometimes quite loudly) how that time was any different. The initial results of the idea obviously fell into the crash-and-burn category, so why was I insisting on moving forward? I wasn't sure I had an answer, but I knew that my gut knew, and at the end of the day, that was what I chose to listen to, and I did. The rest is history. People will come and go, but your gut is your right hand—it is extremely wise and will always stand by your side. The employee of the month award goes to... the *gut*, again!

If you have one person who agrees to believe you have the spark, you are ahead of the game.

An Opportunity for Growth

There may not be a big line of people who will initially understand or support your dream.

A Reason to Celebrate

You don't need a big line of supporters. It only takes one to light the spark.

KNOW PEOPLE WILL MAKE ASSUMPTIONS

The Crying, Flying, and Hard Rock Story

I'm careful about who I spend time with when given a choice. You and I can be friendly, but unless we've shared struggles together or cried together, or you've seen me at my worst, than you've never truly seen me at my best either. Being friendly is a natural, beautiful opportunity you have with every human you meet. Friendship, on the other hand, takes work and time, like a fine painting. The Dot family taught me so much about that.

A few years into Polka Dot Powerhouse's existence, we were exploding with growth. We were flying all over the U.S. to launch chapters. Back in those days, two of us went to each chapter launch. During one trip, my friend Caroline and I traveled together to a launch in Montana. Caroline is one of the most hilarious people I have ever met, and she and I clicked immediately. I was fortunate that she let me see who she truly was from the very beginning, which put me at ease. She is a real person, and she, being so genuinely herself, allowed me to feel safe to do the same. She is another person who has made it easy to breathe. Traveling with her made even the most stressful times fun and joyful. She was an amazing travel mate. This trip had started off wonderfully; Caroline and I had made the ninety-minute trek to the airport, laughing the whole way. The first flight was uneventful. Then we had to wait for the second of two flights that day—a small plane to take us to the town where the launch was being held. As normal terminal business continued around us, Caroline asked, "You going to Carrie's party?"

"What party?" I replied.

"You know. Carrie's party on the 15th. Everyone is going."

"I wasn't invited to any party," I assured her.

What followed was a few moments of confused silence as Caroline and I looked at each other with tilted heads—until it made sense. We both understood what had just happened. I could tell from the look on Caroline's face that she realized she had talked herself into a hole. She always seemed to have a smile on her face, but she didn't at that moment. Feeling a wave of emotion moving through me, I excused myself to the bathroom. I needed a second alone. I felt entirely comfortable with Caroline—we had traveled extensively together, and she had gotten to know not only the shiny parts of me, but also the rough ambivert parts. I knew she saw and accepted me. But, I didn't want to cry in front of all the passengers in the terminal.

Maybe it was travel exhaustion, or maybe it hit me on the wrong day of the month—I'm not sure why exactly, but the minute I closed that stall door, the waterfall started. I sat in that tiny bathroom stall and had a nice, big cry. I bawled because it's hard knowing that launching a big dream can also be so isolating. Even when you're surrounded by people, you can feel completely alone. I cried because I thought Carrie had been a friend of mine, but in that moment, I felt friendless, not worthy to be seen or even accepted anymore—less than. Even though I was headed to a location where I knew people would be excited to see and meet me, it didn't matter in that one moment. I had found out I was no longer important to one of my close personal friends, that she hadn't thought enough of me to invite me to a party all of our other friends had been invited to. So, I had a nice, big, ugly, unapologetic cry. You're darn right I did!

During my twenty-minute bathroom bawl, I listened to person after person enter and exit the other stalls. They were all on their way somewhere and excited to be going. As far as I know, I was the only one in that bathroom crying that day. After about twenty minutes, I pulled myself together, and I returned to the terminal. Caroline stared at me and immediately knew I had been crying. Then she started to cry. There we sat, two professional women on an important business trip, two friends who could feel an open wound oozing all over everyone in Terminal 12. We were two crying women, representing the hurt we all sometimes feel with nowhere to go with those feelings but the small plane we were waiting to board, all while still crying.

Once on board, I simply needed to escape, but there was nowhere to go. I didn't want to talk about it. I didn't want to think about it anymore. I needed an escape. I put in my headphones and turned up the volume as loud as it would go. Hard rock was my choice of genre that day. A few minutes later, I felt a tap on my shoulder. The stewardess was asking me to turn my headphones down or off. It turns out I hadn't inserted the headphone jack into the phone well enough, and the entire plane and everyone on it was getting a dose of my head-banging music. Caroline later told me, "That was so loud, Shannon. *So loud!*" As we flew to our destination, we both continued to quietly cry. I wonder what the other passengers thought. There's no telling.

Once we got to our destination, Caroline revealed to me that the reason she thought I had not been invited to the party is that people hate to bother me because I was always so busy.

I have to admit it was true. I was always running in a million directions and frequently declined invitations in order to devote almost all of my home time to my family. I didn't want to feel I had to attend all the events; I just wanted to know they wanted me there. Isn't that always the case? A true ambivert wants to be invited to the party but doesn't want to have to go. I am indeed a true ambivert.

The moral of this story is that people will make all kinds of assumptions and build stories about who you are, what your life is like, and what your availability is, all without ever checking the accuracy of it. You're sending messages to the world, and people are receiving messages through their own lenses. They may even think you're a snob, or you may have somehow changed based on your dream gaining success. I've learned that this happens to so many founders. Being a founder can be pretty isolating, sometimes by nature and other times by messages we may unconsciously send, or even with walls we may have unintentionally built, but it's there for most of us. Even though you will experience extraordinary joy through launching your dream, isolation is a real thing that must be talked about, mainly because no one seems to be talking about it.

There is nothing you can do about this, except to make sure the message you are sending is the one you want people to receive. Beyond that, you can't control anyone or how they interpret it. You can only control your reactions to what happens.

Just know people will put everything you do through their own lenses. When you start to feel left out or alone, remember that someone may have interpreted your messaging into an untrue story or maybe even a true story. Regardless, whatever conclusion they come to, they likely aren't verifying its accuracy and are proceeding according to their own assumptions.

I've seen people take portions of what I have said or written and misquote me or accuse me of something they know I did not say or do. I used to fight these battles, but I soon realized they were needless distractions that pulled me from the focus required for those I was meant to impact.

It's none of your business what people think of you, but sometimes being reminded that it's quite natural for humans to act like humans who invent stories about you can help you to maneuver around them a bit more effectively.

People always think it's funny when they hear the reference to "the fear of success." Oh, hell yeah, it's real! Success is beautiful and extraordinary but can also be isolating, scary, and lonely. Think of any celebrity you admire, and go look at the comments on their social media pages. People love our success until they don't. Who would intentionally set themselves up for something like that? A big dreamer; that's who! There is a reason that not everyone launches a dream. It can be rough, and not everyone can handle that level of resistance.

People get scared of bright lights, and odds are you are a *neon*, see-it-from-the-moon, amazingly bright light. It's only natural that people won't understand you at times. That's okay. That's actually a compliment to you. You weren't meant to always be understood. You were meant to do big things. Remember that.

An Opportunity for Growth

As the keeper of the dream, people will make all sorts of assumptions about you, your time, and your intentions.

A Reason to Celebrate

People making assumptions is part of the process, and when you understand that, you will be able to handle it better.

DECIDE WHO YOUR FRIENDS ARE

*Not everyone is in your life for the same reason,
but they all have a place.*

I have a habit of keeping people at a distance until I know them better. I also have a habit of falling hard for the people I work with, those who I have worked with on upper leadership, the ones who have been through the muck with me and are still there. I feel safe with them. I lean into them and the comfort of being understood and seen by them. But I am also the boss. It can complicate things.

Sometimes the line between friendly and friends gets blurred.

Every year, our upper leaders have an opportunity to earn a trip with Brian and I to Hawaii. It is our happy place. When I told Brian I wanted to have an incentive trip, Maui was a no-brainer. No one ever complains about Maui. We've been taking the trip for six years now (except for 2020), and it's always full of relaxation, great memories, and joy.

This trip is wonderful every year, but one year in particular delivered a great lesson for me about friends.

During this fabulous trip, I started to feel an unwelcome but familiar feeling around day two. I tried to dismiss it and focus my attention elsewhere, but it didn't work.

As the trip continued, I started to feel like an outcast. I didn't want to feel that way; I was in my happy place with the love of my life and other amazing people, for goodness sakes! Still, those feelings of not being seen in high school came right back. Our trip had a few nighttime group events, but during the days, everyone was on their own. Brian and I spent all of that time together. We soaked up some quality alone time, and it was perfect.

During our daytime journeys, we would come down from our hotel room, and we'd find a big bunch of our fellow attendees hanging out together. *That's great*, I initially thought. Then there would a large group hanging out somewhere else on another day. Huh. About the third day in, we got a call to come down and hang with them—they were grilling in the pool area. Okay, I was wrong; they did want to hang with us. But when we got there, it was obvious to me the call to us had been an afterthought as most of them were done eating. Still, I should have been grateful, right? People were having a great time and connecting. That's the company mission—connection—and it was happening. Part of me was overjoyed. On top of that, I was with Brian. Because we are blessed to be parents of a son with special needs, we don't typically get a lot of time alone. Maui is where we get concentrated time alone. The other attendees knew this, too, so it made sense they would give us our space and time.

So, why was I feeling what I was feeling? I didn't want to feel it. It was ridiculous. Still, it was there; that old familiar feeling of being on the outside was welling up inside me. I didn't even know if we would have accepted an invitation to do something with the larger group during the day since Brian and I were enjoying that one-on-one time. Again, I couldn't help feeling I wanted to be invited. I wanted to know they saw me and that I was of value to them. My true ambivert nature was showing itself once again. I wanted to be invited, regardless of whether I would have gone.

Brian knows me well and could tell I was struggling with conflicting feelings. He supported my right to have whatever feelings I was having, but when I asked him for advice about how I could brush off what I was feeling, he laid down some truth. "Shannon, these are your employees and people who work for you. You are the boss, and no one likes to party with their boss. You are all friendly, and that's great, but you aren't friends." Wow! It took a while for his words to sink in. I hadn't thought of it that way. I hadn't considered how awkward it might be to drink in front of one's boss. I suddenly felt ridiculous and embarrassed for feeling excluded. *Okay*, I thought, *I can be taught. I don't want to mess this up. He's right.* I spent the next several days laying on the beach, googling articles about why a boss shouldn't be friends with employees. Friendly, but not friends. *Alright, I've got it. I can do this.*

When I got back home, I talked to a couple close friends who are not on Polka Dot Powerhouse leadership and who also own truly impactful businesses and are doing big things in the world. Both of them agreed with Brian. One said, "Yeah, bosses and employees can get along great, but they really can't be friends as it is a recipe for problems." How could I have had it so wrong for so long? Why was I just learning this? What hadn't someone told me? Employers and employees can't be friends?!? It appeared to be an unspoken rule everyone knew except for me, at least until that trip.

Only, that concept didn't feel quite right either. I had worked with some of those people for a long time, and they had helped me build the company; they were definitely friends. We had traveled to spend downtime together outside of work. Some of them were very vested in my family and in my life. A few of us even had each other on cell tracking devices in case of an emergency. As far as I'm concerned, if you and someone else have the ability to track each other's phones in case of emergencies, that person is considered a friend.

So, what was I to do? Can a boss be friends with those they work with? The logic of friendly but not friends made all kinds of sense and was "appropriate" for a workplace, but it also didn't fully fit my situation, and it likely may not fit yours either. I really didn't know what to do. Out of desperation and the need to make some sense of it all, I invented a barometer to gauge the situation.

First, you won't be friends with everyone, regardless of whether they work with you, and that is the way it's supposed to be. With some, you will simply have a friendly working relationship, and there is nothing wrong with that. With others, you will be friendly and enjoy each other's company. You may know more about them than other employees, but you wouldn't do anything with them outside of work or wouldn't know much about their lives outside of work. There's nothing wrong with that either. With a select few, you may build a genuine friendship capable of continuing with or without the current working situation, one that could possibly last a season or a lifetime. There's nothing wrong with that. Others may disagree with me, but I don't think you can plunk everyone in a neat box that's one-size-fits-all. That doesn't make much sense to me.

People are simply overwhelmed with reasons and seasons and stories. The day after I sold the magazine, my Facebook friends list dropped by 200 people—200! I didn't have a fight with anyone, I hadn't changed my life philosophy or values, and I hadn't committed any crimes or wound up in the paper. My title simply changed from owner and editor to previous owner and editor. I cannot tell you who the 200 people were (which probably reveals a lot about our importance to each other), but whoever they were, they knew me as Shannon Crotty, magazine owner and editor, and when that was no longer the case, my association to them and their lives ended. I think, especially for women, that type of thing can feel like a sucker punch, but the truth is, your life is like a great big storage bin. When it gets too full, there isn't room for anything or anyone else. New opportunities and new people are always trying to reach us, so sometimes it's necessary for God or the Universe to clean out the bin to make room for who and what's trying to get in.

My friend Alice always says we have friends for a reason, a season, or a lifetime. Not everyone is meant to be there forever. That's by design, and while it may not feel like it, it is a huge blessing.

No matter how long someone is in your life, it is the perfect amount of time. Everything is moving in perfect timing based on who you are as a person in that moment. Whether you are coworkers, friendly, or true friends, embrace them all. All of the people you encounter while launching and protecting the dream, or those in your personal life, are there to provide value, lessons, and joy. You can love them all and know how valuable they are not only to the dream, but also to you as a person. If you have connected with someone in your life, see their value, and know it is a gift, for however long it lasts. I love that.

An Opportunity for Growth

Not everyone you see or work with will be your friend, and sometimes it will take effort to figure out how they fit into your life.

A Reason to Celebrate

Everyone, whether they are friendly, your friend, or none of the above, plays a role in your life and the life of your dream. Be grateful for each one of those people.

YOU'RE GOING TO NEED SOME ALLIES

To sit with those who understand your journey is a miraculous thing.

One of the reasons that being the keeper of the dream can be so isolating is because complaints travel up the ladder, not down. I'm not suggesting it should go otherwise; this is exactly how it should be. Complaints should always go up—never down.

The only thing about that is if you're the boss and the keeper of the dream, who do you talk to? Who do you get support from? Who do you sort out feelings and experiences with in your journey?

One person I choose to do that with is Brian, but he and I are polar opposites. Where I'm driven by the mission and vision, he is driven by the numbers, the spreadsheets, and the bottom line. We make a great team, one that's able to look at a situation from all angles. That being said, men and women are mentally built different, and as grateful as I am for him, it's sometimes nice to have another woman to compare notes with, too.

I highly recommend you find a group of positive friends who are not directly involved with your dream. We have created a one-of-a-kind opportunity to do that in Polka Dot Power-house. Thousands of women across the globe are all helping, supporting, and pushing each other to be the best and highest versions of themselves. It is truly unlike any other community I have ever experienced, and I am so proud of it.

Being able to lean into the relationships I've built for support in Polka Dot Powerhouse has changed my life.

I also found a great release in a writing group called the Cheetah Mastermind, created with three other long-term friends. It popped up organically when I first started thinking about writing this book. They were all in the process of or wanting to write books or blogs. One of them suggested we should meet once a month on Zoom to compare notes, and bada bing! We were on our way. It started as a monthly writing mastermind, but we always wound up talking about life, so it really transformed into a life mastermind. Although the group has evolved, and we no longer meet monthly, I still regularly lean on them for support through an online app.

You can also find additional support through sports or hobbies you have. I am a fairly new golfer, but I love the sport. The season I started, I decided to jump in with both feet and dedicated to making a commitment to the sport, so I joined a local women's league. I put a call out on social media to see who wanted to join me. The Untamed golf team was formed. There is a lot of laughing and cursing in golf, and it gives me a few hours a week when all I focus on is myself and getting better at golf. It is a darn good release!

In addition, we also have a diamond-level membership in Polka Dot Powerhouse. The women on this level can participate in amazing small and large group masterminds that have transformed the way people do business and support each other, both professionally and personally.

My point here is whether it's an extraordinary family like Polka Dot Powerhouse, your partner, a sports group, a master-mind, a crafting group, or basically anything that makes you happy, be sure to find release, comfort, and support. Set the intention for more allies, and watch as they flow in. They are definitely looking for you as an ally, too.

An Opportunity for Growth

Being a founder and keeper of the dream can, at times, be lonely and isolating.

A Reason to Celebrate

There are allies all around you. Look for them; they are there.

CONSULT EXPERTS BUT LISTEN TO YOUR GUT

There's a lot of voices but only one true north.

During the first two or three years as the founder of Polka Dot Powerhouse, I was running scared. I wanted someone—*anyone!*—to tell me what to do. I didn't want to mess up this beautiful gift, and I was sure I was going to.

Being in such a desperate state, I was willing to listen to anyone who seemed to know what they were doing. While I'm normally stingy on trust, I felt I had no choice but to say, "Help me!" when I ran into someone with experience.

The early days of Polka Dot Powerhouse found us working with several experts. Some of them helped us, and others hurt us. I felt they all had wonderful intentions and truly wanted to help us, but the problem was we weren't all on the same page with what the vision of Polka Dot Powerhouse was. They were giving us advice and guidance based on other companies they had worked with, but I never entertained the idea of making sure it fit our mission, and usually it did not.

We heard and experienced it all—trying to change our company colors to their favorite colors, keeping me hidden at events, telling me I had to look a certain way and pretend to be something I wasn't. I could go on and on.

I can't tell you how much momentum we lost by following every piece of advice handed to us, but it was a significant amount.

The advice I was given was sound and had worked for other large and growing companies, but most of it didn't work for us, and I eventually gained the confidence, courage, and clarity to take advice, put it through our filter of vision and mission, and politely decline when it didn't complement who we are and what our mission is.

One of the most important things you'll have to do as the keeper of the dream is to protect it from experts who may be trying to help but who don't understand your dream the way you think they should. How do you do that? The answer is your gut.

Your gut will be all things. Your gut knows the answers all the time. Sometimes we can't hear the gut through all of the noise, but it's always there. Sometimes it's a quiet whisper, and sometimes it's a fire siren. Whether it's hard to hear or is screaming loudly in your ear, you can be sure your gut knows the path forward. Sometimes that will mean taking good advice, and sometimes that will mean hearing advice and declining it.

You can trust your gut as you would your closest confidant, your best friend, your soul mate, your parent. It is all of these things wrapped up with a beautiful bow.

If you don't know what your gut sounds like, get quiet and listen.

It can take practice. If it feels too overwhelming, start slowly—get quiet for a minute or two a day and build on that.

I can tell you the only time I could hear my gut when we started was when I was alone in the quiet. Over time, I have learned how my gut speaks, and I can now hear it over others and even through all the noise.

You may not think it's true, but your gut is already talking to you and waiting for you to listen. Your beautiful gut will get you out of trouble, save you time, and bring you joy.

So, by all means, ask opinions, seek expert advice, and truly listen when given advice. But before you make any big decisions based on that advice, I hope you first give it to your gut for input. You will not be sorry.

An Opportunity for Growth

It will be easy to get turned sideways by the advice you will be given.

A Reason to Celebrate

Advice is a really good thing, as long as you first pass it through your gut and your mission and vision filters.

ACKNOWLEDGE THOSE WHO IMPACT

Everyone wants to be seen. A simple nod in their direction makes a world of difference.

I used to have a bad habit of forgetting to acknowledge people I had intended to acknowledge. It drove me crazy, but it was admittedly not enough for me to take immediate action to find a solution. It took me years.

Remember how I said you should not simply wish and think about things but that the key is taking action and actually scheduling important things? There is no place this is truer than how you acknowledge others.

Believe me. I know what it's like to want to give acknowledgement to so many but run out of hours in the day to get done all the things I want to do.

I am certainly guilty of going to bed exhausted, lying there preparing to sleep and remembering there was someone I intended and really wanted to acknowledge but forgot to do so. *You gotta remember to do that tomorrow, Shannon.* I'm blessed to have an extraordinary assistant who has many strengths I don't understand, and she helps me remember to do the things that are important to me. But when I'm left to my own devices, I often drop the ball. Remember, I'm not a detail person, so the details of intent often get past me.

In addition to my amazing assistant helping me out, I finally got sick of not remembering to acknowledge people and developed a system to help myself. I have a list for acknowledgement. As someone makes an impression on me or strikes a chord in my heart, they go onto the list. As I add them to my list, I immediately decide how I am going to acknowledge them, and I make an appointment in my calendar for a date and time to do just that.

How I decide to acknowledge people varies. I try to ask revealing questions when I talk to people, although it is not always the same question. Through the questions I ask them or from what I observe on social media or in person, I try to make the acknowledgement and send the message that I see them as a unique individual and that I took the time to listen to what makes them, *them*. Maybe it's a small item they collect or a book I think will mean something to them. Sometimes it's simply a token that has their favorite color or reminds them of something they told me about their past. I send a fair amount of poker tokens that can calm an anxious mind while traveling or an angel token for someone who is grieving. A lot of the time, it's simply a handwritten card letting people know I am thinking of them.

In addition to my own list, we keep a list of people in the Dot family who our leaders hear may need a nod of congratulations, support, or a note saying, "I'm thinking of you."

People don't care how you acknowledge them; it doesn't have to be big or expensive or take too much time. People simply want to know they matter to you and that their lives make a difference. They want to know you see them. They need to know that you do.

An Opportunity for Growth

You will never be able to acknowledge every person who needs acknowledgement.

A Reason to Celebrate

You can set a regular schedule to acknowledge those you can and to let them know they are important.

USE THE GRATITUDE GOODBYE EXERCISE

Everyone with whom you come into contact plays a role in your story. You at least owe them a proper goodbye.

Growing up with my dad wasn't easy. My dad, J.D., was six-feet, four-inches of pure charm. People were drawn to him. People looked at our family, and they seemed to get sucked into how great it must have been to have my father as a dad. It was not. My dad was great at messaging, but only in the genre of fiction. Real life bore no resemblance to the messaging he was sending. I know my father put out the image of who he truly wanted to be, but once he got home and was with my mom, my sister, and me, that person floated away. I truly believe my dad meant well—God rest his soul—but somewhere along the line, my dad, one of eight children, formed anxiety and dysfunction around responsibility, so much so that he just couldn't handle it.

My mom loved new things, and my dad loved to get them for her, whether we could afford them or not. So, my mom and dad would acquire things and more things. Things would stack up all around us, all while my father's big plans and employment would either be a straight-out lie, or they would fall apart. He would start making promises to people, including us, that he couldn't keep, and the pressure would build. You could feel that pressure building and knew what was coming. One day, we would come home from school, and Dad would be gone. No note, no call, no Dad. Where would he go? I don't know, but it was far away. Once he was gone, all his lies would come to light, and my mom, my sister, and I would start cleaning up the mess. We would sell everything, battle the creditors, and move again. My mom would usually have two or three jobs, just trying to pull everything back around. After a year or two of pure survival, we'd start to see light at the end of the tunnel. We could see the blinding light of hope shining through. We could breathe again. And just like that (wouldn't you know it), as if he had a sixth sense that we were once again on solid ground, my dad would show up and want to come home. And that would be the first day of the cycle starting all over, the cycle that would repeat over and over again throughout my childhood and adolescence.

My father and my sister fought outwardly a lot about "the cycle," but I battled it more internally, or at least more than they did. Regardless, my dad and I had a turbulent relationship. I was never able to trust him. My mom was always hoping he would choose to change, but I knew he was living a habitual cycle from which he could not break free. He wanted to, I am sure, as my dad had a really good heart, but he didn't know how.

Only after he and my mom retired, and the burden of having to provide for a family no longer existed, did my mom and dad find stability and peace together.

At the time of my dad's passing in 2007, my father and I were civil and pleasant with each other, but it was still an uncomfortable relationship. We were sorting through thirty-eight years of trash and trauma, and we didn't have nearly enough time to get through it all.

I remember the day he passed; it was from a massive heart attack. We knew it was coming. The doctors knew he had a lot of blockage from years of chain smoking, but he was, at the time, on dialysis and very sick from years of undiagnosed diabetes, so he was not healthy enough to do anything to prevent what was coming. On the day he died, they led us back to where they had been working on him in the emergency room. He lay there dead. He was no longer scary to me. I no longer disliked him. I no longer wanted to yell and scream at him. I simply remember stroking his hair and telling him over and over again that I loved him and that more than anything, I wished we had been given more time.

When we went home, and over the following week or two, I was a certifiable mess. I know it must have confused those in my life. My dad and I weren't close. As far as they knew, we didn't even like each other. Why was I so upset? I could not explain it to anyone or even to myself. I once heard Tony Robbins say, "If you're going to blame someone for all the bad things, you've got to blame them for the good, too." I legitimately had a lot to blame my dad for. There were plenty of bad things he did that no one would blame me for pointing the finger at him for, but when I looked at the situation through grown-up and grief-stained eyes, I could see there was also good. While I hated to admit it while he was alive, my dad had a lot to do with me becoming the person I became. He and the messed-up world we lived in helped to create many of the attributes I love most about myself. And that was my first experience with the grateful goodbye exercise. I needed something to help me heal from the loss of his death, so I sat down and wrote my dad a letter that I never shared with anyone. It wasn't for them. It was simply for my dad and for me.

I have used the process of that letter since, every time someone significant in my life was no longer there, whether by fate, their choice, or mine. When someone I know, have become close to, or have worked with for a while leaves, I give them a little ceremony. They never know it. This exercise is for me; part of my morning ritual is saying goodbye to anyone I need to.

This powerful exercise helps me remain in gratitude. It helps me be able to continue to trust. It is a source for me to seek new opportunities with people. It is a gift.

It not only works for people, but also for situations and dreams.

I don't know about you, but when I'm done with something or someone, I am completely done. It's not that I'm bitter or angry. I don't wish anything bad on anyone; I'm just done.

Back when we sold the magazine, I had already been mentally done for quite a while. Once Polka Dot Powerhouse walked into my life, I found it was all I wanted to do. I still loved the magazine and the crutch it provided me, but I had been mentally gone for several months before it sold.

Once the sale was complete, I had to force myself to read any publications, even that one. It wasn't about being mad or bitter, but I had given every ounce of what I had to it, and my mind just said I was done.

I don't think I'm alone with being completely done and wanting absolutely nothing to do with something once it's done, either out of sheer exhaustion or because things simply ran their course. I think more people than not are like that.

I also think the people-pleasing little girl in me always equated someone leaving with me doing something wrong, making someone mad, or not being enough. Lord knows I still have my days, but I am not that person anymore. I now know that people leave for their own reasons. Those reasons sometimes involve me, and other times they don't. If you're going to make an assumption, make the assumption of the best possibility—of positivity and of purpose. If you're going to assume anything, assume someone is leaving your life, a project, your staff, or as a client because it is, for whatever reason, no longer in alignment with who they are at that moment—possibly for who you are as well.

People evolve and change. Priorities shift and move. You will also attract different people, whether as a person or as a founder, as you change and grow. It is inevitable. There is no use in chasing people or shaming ourselves over someone else's choices. I know that is easier said than done. Those darn habits don't want to go down quietly. That's why I developed the Gratitude Goodbye Exercise for myself.

For me, it starts with writing a thank-you note to them. In the thank-you note, I express all the things I liked about them and how they improved my life. I thank them for the lessons they taught me and, if applicable, the time and passion they contributed to a project, the Polka Dot Powerhouse community, or me. And I thank them again.

If the person leaves on good and pleasant terms, I send them the thank-you note in the mail. If they don't, I usually toss it in the garbage.

The next step holds more goodness in the interest of clarity and knowledge. For each person I write a thank-you note to—whether or not I send it—I also write about my experience with them on my writing pad. I write a solid page in a specific folder, specifically for this purpose. I rewrite what I appreciate about them and what I am thankful for in them, but I also write the lessons I learned from them and how I will use those lessons moving forward, so I don't make the same mistakes again in the future. I also sometimes write why it makes sense that this person is no longer involved and also why I think it's time for us both to move on.

Then I take a moment to engineer the idea of who or what opportunity I would like to have fill this new, open space. Think of that storage bin. When it becomes too full, it will naturally get cleaned out to make room for a new person or opportunity.

After I've completed that, I turn the paper over or go to a second sheet in the writing pad and do the exact same exercise for myself. I won't be the same person I was when this person entered my life, and that change needs to be respected, too. I thank myself, recognize the lessons I learned, and engineer what I wish my next evolution to be. It's not that I need to change, but we all have areas we wish to improve in. There is power in writing all this down.

This is a very powerful activity.

How does this benefit the keeper of the dream? First, it is a nice release, a form of self-care therapy, if you will.

Second, and as I have mentioned before, there is power in writing things down. When I intentionally look for the reason, the lesson, and the blessing in someone's departure, it helps me to pay them a silent level of gratitude while I also learn and grow.

Respect, knowledge, and understanding—you can never get too much of that. It is what we're all seeking in life. To do this exercise when it is needed is a sign of love to both your experience with them and to yourself and the role you played.

That's a really good thing.

An Opportunity for Growth

Goodbyes are hard.

A Reason to Celebrate

Goodbyes are an important and consistent part of life, and there is a way to deal with them that helps us grow.

A PARTING NOTE

I see you, the keeper of the dream.

I know how important you are, and I hope you get that, too.

You are most certainly on your own journey, and that is a tremendous gift.

I know I in no way covered all the tricks and hacks you'll need to survive on this journey, but I hope reading this book made you feel seen, understood, and respected.

I hope you learned one or two things to take with you on this incredible journey that will lead you to impact so many people; we cannot even see how far your ripple goes. That just gives me chills.

I hope that knowing you are not alone—never alone—in this journey helps you to find the courage to dream bigger, live bolder, and be unapologetically more of yourself, for you are perfect, and the world needs more of who you truly are.

I see you and I appreciate you. I know what you're doing is not easy, but it's worthy of your work, sacrifice, and tears because it is meant to make a difference in the lives of so many people. For that, I applaud you. Keep going, even when it's hard. Keep going, even when you're not sure. Keep going, even when you feel alone. The dream needs you. Those who will be impacted by the dream need you.

It won't always be easy, but it will be worth it.

You're worth it.

With love,
Your fellow visionary,
Shannon

ACKNOWLEDGEMENTS

Thank you to my handsome husband, Brian, for everything you do and are. The gift of building a life with you brings me immense joy. The day God brought you into my life was the day he sent me my life's greatest blessing and the greatest single lesson on what an extraordinary love is and how it can change everything. I love you more.

Thank you to my extraordinary children, Bailey, TJ, Zach, and James (my bonus son). You help me keep my heart grounded and my soul soaring. You inspire me to always continue improving myself and to be a better human, even though I know you love me as I am. My greatest and proudest accomplishment is that I was chosen to be your mom. I love you more.

Thank you to my sister, Tina. She was and remains my very best friend. Even from heaven, she continues to be a source of inspiration and motivation for me and has sent me so many amazing sisters. I love you.

Thank you to my parents, Judy and Jerry (J.D.), for loving me and believing in me. I owe so much of who I am to all of the lessons I learned from you. I am so grateful you were chosen to be my parents. I love you.

Thank you to my in-laws, Cynthia and Calvin, for being wonderful parents and grandparents to our whole family. I love you.

Thank you to my sister-in-law, Debra, for introducing me to your brother. That one simple act changed my life. I love you.

Thank you to my extended family. Every one of you has played a role in me becoming who I am. I am sending a big hug and love to you.

Thank you to my extraordinary executive assistant and friend, Anna. I do not know how I functioned before you came into my life, but I am so grateful for you. I love you.

Thank you to the many leaders with whom I have had the blessing of working, especially the Polka Dot Powerhouse Legacy Leaders. It is an honor to know you and to work so closely with you to spread sisterhood across the globe. I am in awe of you.

Thank you to every Polka Dot Powerhouse member—past, present, and future. You have all played such an important role in the Polka Dot Powerhouse legacy, and each and every one of you is important, respected, and loved.

Thank you to Cora for being the very first paying Polka Dot Powerhouse member, even though you had no idea at the time. It takes just one to light a spark, and your action kept me going when everything else was telling me to quit.

Thank you for everyone who encouraged me or had a hand in helping me process, write, or produce this book. There are so many people, but especially Shawna Stanley, Tristine Davis, Alice Rothbauer, Michele (One-L) Paquette, Chelle Barnaby, Gretchen Frana, Mercedes Wharton, K. Paige Engle, Suzanne Moore, Danielle Anderson, and Kirsten "Kiki" Ringer.

Thank you to all those I have been honored to call friends. Being close with people requires me to push beyond my comfort zone, but I am always overjoyed to do it for you. Thank you for seeing me. I am sending love to you all.

Thank you to everyone who ever said something positive, nice, or encouraging to me. I heard every word, and it made a difference in my life, even if you didn't know it at the time.

Thank you to everyone who was critical, not nice, or simply didn't like me. You taught me so many lessons that strengthened me as a person. You helped me gain clarity, boundaries, standards, and a true love of myself.

Finally, I want to thank me for never giving up on myself and my dreams. Thank you for learning to use fear as fuel. I love you, Shannon, and I always will. Keep going.

ABOUT THE AUTHOR

Shannon Crotty is a wife and mom of three who lives in West Central Wisconsin. She is the Founder and CEO of Polka Dot Powerhouse, a global connection company for women. You can learn more about Polka Dot Powerhouse at polkadotpowerhouse.com.

Shannon is also the founder and visionary of The Deep End Planner, a great accompaniment to this book. You can learn more about The Deep End Planner at shannoncrotty.com.

Also, as a sought-after speaker, Shannon not only empowers audiences to be more authentic versions of themselves, but she also provides tools for them to rein in their focus to allow them to more easily reach their goals and launch their dreams.

Shannon loves golfing, travel, style, fitness, and the good ice. You can learn more about Shannon at shannoncrotty.com.

Made in the USA
Monee, IL
29 March 2023

30772943R00090